MW01265439

FACT/DISCLAIMER

During the latter part of the 20th century a writer/producer named Larry David co-created a fabulously successful comedy television series by the name of *It's All About Nothing (Seinfeld)* and later starred in his own series, *It's All About Me (Curb Your Enthusiasm)*. They were tremendous hits and made Larry into a mega-millionaire and true comedy icon.

I adore that Larry David. I watched him during his pre-icon days on the Catch a Rising Star stage in New York City where his clever, sometimes peculiar material may have not received roaring approval from the comedy club audience, but it got me. It got me right in the place that vindicated risk. He was special and I knew it the first moment I saw him. As he grew into a larger than life (due to a suspected growth hormone), the architect of unique comedy programming that drew immense following, I realized that even the most personal work can touch the masses.

THIS BOOK IS NOT ABOUT THAT LARRY DAVID.

Though based on a true story, this book is a purely fabricated account of a character whose life closely mimics that of the nonfictional Larry David. In effect, this story takes place in a universe where some people and events may seem similar to the world you live in (in some cases names may appear to look like the real names, but I assure you, the pronunciations are completely different and any actions attributed to them are purely metaphors), but despite what might be your distorted view of reality, this story involves characters and events purely fictional.

In fact, even though you are reading this today, which is not 2005, the story you are reading takes place in early 2005 around a year and a half before the middle of 2006.

THE
LARRY DAVID
CODE

A Pretty, Pretty Good Novel

STEVE YOUNG

The Larry David Code: A Pretty, Pretty Good Novel
©Steve Young

ISBN 979-8-35096-421-9 (print)
ISBN 979-8-35095-782-2 (eBook)

Dedicated to

Richard Lewis

A Special Comedian and Friend

ACKNOWLEDGEMENTS

I know I'm going to leave out a number of names who played important parts in making this book happen, especially those who took the time to read earlier drafts that I guilted them into doing as it is the last thing any writer wants to do. Assume that if I haven't mentioned your name you still played an significant role in making this book happen.

Some I remember are Elliott Curson, Chip Keyes, Richard Lewis, Cathy Ladman, Andy Cowan, Rick Overton, Anita Wise and Dennis Palumbo.

But most important, there is no question that if it wasn't for Larry David canceling our interviews… well, the following pages would have never been written.

Larry, you da man!

CONTENTS

Preface..1

Chapter 1. Bam 4

Chapter 2. A Few Days Before..6

Chapter 3. Fuck...8

Chapter 4. A LITTLE Bit About Me 10

Chapter 5. Larry* 12

Chapter 6. Interview Insolvency..18

Chapter 7. Getting Back to Getting Back at Larry 22

Chapter 8. Hello Larry..25

Chapter 9. Goodbye Larry 32

Chapter 10. Too Funny, Too Fat 41

Chapter 11. On The Run 45

Chapter 12. Something Smells Like H: HBO 50

Chapter 13. What Does GO 27000 Mean?..............................57

Chapter 14. The Writers Guild – Jobs 'Rn't Us 60

Chapter 15. Meanwhile, Back in the Jungle............................72

Chapter 16. Another One Bites the Dust................................78

Chapter 17. Groaning, I mean, Groening................................84

Chapter 18. Beverly Hills Celebrity Task Force........................86

Chapter 19. Groening Goes on Eternal Hiatus........................89

Chapter 20. Clank...93

Chapter 21. The Nixon Library 96

Chapter 22. I Mean, **HE** Was Larry David 100

Chapter 23. 9-11: Revisited..109

Chapter 24. Being Drafted into Larry's Army..115

Chapter 25. It Hits the Fan...126

Chapter 26. Ztivo...130

Chapter 27. Not Again...132

Chapter 28. Contrived, Thy Name Be Me..138

Chapter 29. God. Discuss...144

Chapter 30. Clean Up, Aisle Illch..149

Chapter 31. Par le vous Burbank..160

Chapter 32. Y'Got Company..166

Chapter 33. The Flight...169

Chapter 34. Bienvenue a Paris...170

Chapter 35. It Was an Exceptionally Uneventful Life.......................177

Chapter 36. Resurrection...188

Chapter 37. Crash Aftermath: The Movie 190

Chapter 38. Damanhur...196

Chapter 39. Chuck DeGaulle Airport Terminal…
       Very Terminal...199

Chapter 40. We'll Always Have Paree..201

Chapter 41. On The Way Out from Whence I Came......................205

Chapter 42. Can't Think of a Decent Chapter Title 208

Chapter 43. On the Way to Mandalay..214

Chapter 44. Fast Times at Paris High...217

Chapter 45. Syndicated Escape..220

Chapter 46. Lourving Art..222

Chapter 47. It All Came Down to This 251

Chapter 48. The Long Story...256

Chapter 49. So That I Don't Get a Bad Yelp Rating 257

Epilogue..267

PREFACE

"When television is good, nothing—not the theater, not the magazines, not newspapers—nothing is better. But when television is bad, nothing is worse. I invite each of you to sit down in front of your own television set when your station goes on the air and stay there, for a day, without a book, without a magazine, without a newspaper, without a profit and loss sheet or a rating book to distract you. Keep your eyes glued to that set until the station signs off (ancient reference). I can assure you that what you will observe is a vast wasteland. You will see a procession of game shows, formula comedies about totally unbelievable families, blood and thunder, mayhem, violence, sadism, murder, western bad men, western good men, private eyes, gangsters, more violence, and cartoons. And endless commercials—many screaming, cajoling, and offending. And most of all, boredom. True, you'll see a few things you will enjoy. But they will be very, very few. And if you think I exaggerate, I only ask you to try it." Newton Minow, Federal Communications Commission (FCC) chairman, May 9, 1961

Have you ever wondered how or why network television continues to produce so much mindless crap?*[1] There are exceptions. Only kidding. There aren't. They are more what the industry refers technically to as "flukes." Quality sometimes squeaks through, but only when a network makes a deal with a producer icon and the network honchos figure they can ride some sort of *The Producer Who Brought You Your Last Hit* marketing cache (see:

1 *It might have changed since, but at this printing the crap continues.*

Chuck Lorre). This sets up a small window where the *showrunning* (boss) producer gets the opportunity to actually take a risk. Truth be known, or at least leaked, risk is something the network bigwigs would never risk. Too much of a risk. It's the CYA hypothesis and their asses are much too valuable to them to gamble on someone else's courage.

Others creative projects get on the schedule due to what some call "for crissakes, I swear I didn't know there were any more copies of that video" motivation. Unless you're Kim Kardashian, private tape stash is better burned than distributed. Believe me I know – thank you Mr. Way Too Much D & D (drug and drink).

There are plenty of stated reasons for bad shows. Some say it's because there is no imagination in network management. That's not true. Kidding again. It is true. The last time these *people* used their imagination was when they imagined they could be writers. They're much more interested in what they think will work.*₂ And they fail miserably at that. The math proves it.

About a day after a network decides what will go on the new schedule, programs that the powers-to-be will proudly promote as potential hits at the annual TV critics' conclave, they begin the search for the next season's shows to replace almost all of the shows they have promoted proudly to be this season's hits.

Here's how it (doesn't) works. A producer/writer pitches an idea to the network. About three hundred of these ideas are deemed brilliant enough by the network to give it a go or what is known as: putting it into *development*. This is also known as *development hell*. They're interchangeable. Still, at this point, the writer's concept is allowed to be imaginative, even, heart be still, clever.

Money is given to the writer to expand the idea into a pilot script. The writer goes home and excuses his family, if he's old enough to have one, from his life. Then after a few hundred, give or take, drafts and getting feedback from friends he trusts*₃, he turns it in to the network.

At this point, about one hundred producers get their pilots ordered and shot.

Without going through the entire process in which the *hell* part of *development hell* is permanently affixed, some fifty new shows get named to the new fall (or as Fox puts it, *anytime*) schedule.

Are you following me? So far fifty of the three hundred concepts, which the *smart* guys and gals at the network get beaucoup bucks to say will or won't work, are already working at about an 84% failure rate or what the network likes to call, "a 100% success of what didn't fail." Here's where it really becomes fun. Of those fifty shows that make it on to the schedule, about twenty will not be canceled and make it to the following year's schedule. Of those, maybe five, if that, will stay on and perhaps be considered *hits*. So, the original three hundred, deemed brilliant enough by the network to give it a go, are now five. That's a 98.4% failure rate or what the network heads like to call... Well, they don't call it anything because the ones in charge of calling it anything have long since been sacked to utilize their failure experience to form their own production companies or leave the industry altogether to get back into law or used car sales where they feel they can really do something beneficial for humankind.

You can do the numbers yourself. It's really quite titillating. Point is, they do this over and over and never seem to learn.

Or is it that they choose not to?

---

3 *These are people in close proximity of the producer who pray that the writer/producer's script gets made, that they might get hired on his/her staff. If the show does not get picked up these friends will stop reading the writer's scripts, unless he picks up their checks at Art's Deli.*

CHAPTER ONE

Bam

BAM!

A gunshot ... or a car's backfire. Of course, it could have been both a gunshot and a backfire happening simultaneously, a contrived scenario much like the moment a sitcom character alludes to "the one thing that would never happen," and much to the surprise (not) to the viewer – wait for it – it does.

Bam!

Another gun shot? No, that was definitely a backfire. I have got to find some mechanic I can trust[*4] to look at that. That's about the fifth or sixth time I thought someone was shooting at me.

Christ. I'm staked out in front of the mega-mansion owned by the celebrated Larry David, just hoping I might be able to snag that long-awaited magazine interview I pined for. Now I'm just stinking up the place with explosions produced by a running internal combustion engine that occurs in the air intake or exhaust system rather than inside the combustion chamber, which could be the result of a lie perpetrated by the George W. Bush administration. Wikipedia is such a great source for car repair information.

---

4 *An enigma so universally pondered that Webster's added to the word's definition, "man's hopeless search for an honest auto mechanic who spurns using 'you're lucky you made it in here alive' prior to overcharging for a repair that was unnecessary."*

I turned off the engine.

Pow!

Now that's a gun shot.

Shit!

After waiting the prerequisite fifteen minutes that might allow the actual danger to diminish adequately before I checked out the source of the blast, I jumped out of my car. My heady prudence came coincidentally from a suggestion my friend Prudence – "Pru" to friends and would-be lovers – who once revealed to me the secret that had prevented me from putting courage ahead of safety.

"The only thing worse than an unemployed writer: A dead unemployed writer."

I cautiously snuck around to the back of Larry's house where the tallest penguin I'd ever seen raced out and climbed – s*tumbled* more than climbed – into a waiting car. I soon realized it wasn't a penguin at all, but a tuxedoed Michael Richards, who played the venerable Kramer Cosmo of *Seinfeld* fame whose character's signature was some variation of a back or forward fall through Jerry's door. He was sweating so much that if he had charcoal covering his face it would have dripped off leaving an ebony trail running up to the skid marks left by the getaway Fiat that roared off into the dark.

I moved to the window and what I saw sent a shock through my entire body. In the middle of a large opulent bedroom sat an enormous, netted divan. Almost swallowed up by a bevy of large, fluffy and vibrant colored pillows lay a blood-spattered Larry David, eyes rolled back into the pieces of what remained of his blood-soaked skull.

I couldn't help thinking that something was wrong.

CHAPTER TWO

A Few Days Before

It was opening day for Casey, my eight-year-old son's Little League season. This would be his best year. We had worked all off-season on his swing. Last year he had a hitch where he would upper cut on every pitch. But now he had a perfect, level swing. I had basically fashioned a Craftsman 3 vial I-beam level that attached to his bat so that we would know the very moment he was square with the ground. Yep. Level as level could be. The kind that delivered line drives with every bat-to-ball connection.

Sweet.

My daughter was in seventh heaven. She had sold more Girl Scout cookies than anyone in her troop. Broke records. The computer mail program (a hybrid mix of Facebook, Snip-Snap, LinkedIn, Google and Pornmunch.com) I developed reached every relative, friend and friend of a friend around the world. Key was my link to every "10 Best *Britain's Best Talent*" YouTube videos, accumulating a plethora of orders with a single "push *enter*, please." The local paper came to take pictures and Kelly was as giddy as giddy could be.

The cortisone shot given to the woman I had hired to act as my wife had provided her with nearly a full week of relief from her pole dancing accident. The police were unable to determine why the dancer hit her with that pole. The pain would eventually return. It always did. In a few days I would have to suffer through her suffering again, but for today the shot had done its work. What a sight to see her in the kitchen, wearing only an apron and nothing else. Unfortunately, the apron was a full-length wrap-around. She whistled that Tom Jones song ("After the Lovin") she loved so (Wait a minute. It was Engelbert Humperdinck she loved. Not the German composer… the singer) as she baked a room full of cookies: Chocolate chip with a hint of almonds. My favorite.

Above all, the day's grand flavor was piqued by my own work effort. I had garnered an interview with the one writer/producer who I considered the savviest in the business, the one who had inspired me to go into writing in the first place… Larry David. My work for a TV/film industry magazine didn't pay all that well but did present me with the opportunity to meet many of the most prolific scribes in film and television. In one more day we would be doing the interview. I had always wondered how someone so unique, so seemingly unaffected in the ways of networking, so absolutely contrary to what I had thought was needed to become a success, had fashioned a killer career. He was unique. He was hysterically clever. He was, in short, my hero.

All was right with the world.

And then, the phone rang.

It was Larry.

"I can't do the interview."

CHAPTER THREE

Fuck

"What?"

"I can't do it," Larry repeated, though with less resolve.

I wanted to explode. At the very least call my sponsor. But I realized times like this were the very thing I struggled to get sober *⁵ for. Sober for? Well, in the least, it could rationalize ending a sentence with a preposition. Yet beginning a sentence with a conjunction would always be a no-go.

As I knew from reading so many self-improvement books, smeared with pounds of yellow-highlighted sentences that instructed me to take positive action, I had to stop to have a wee bit of a conversation with myself.

Hold on, Steve. Relax. I'm sure you'll work it out. It's just another one of those little life bumps. Larry must have a good reason. Ask him. It could change your entire perspective.

"Larry. Why can't you do it?"

"I just can't."

Fucker.

"But Lar. We had this planned for five months."

"I'm sorry."

---

5 *I had to get sober. I'll never forget the night I was so loaded that I walked into an Olive Garden and thought it was an Italian restaurant.*

"You're sorry? That's all you have to say? You're sorry. For crissakes, Larry. You make $50 million a month and I'll be lucky to make $500 on this interview. It's not like I can't use the money. I've been pitching ideas for shows and movies for almost ten years and made a pittance. You fart and HBO pays you a million to develop the smell. C'mon, I need this gig."

"Steve, if I would do an interview with anyone it would be you."

"And what bank is going to take that deposit?"

"I gotta go."

"Wait. How about bringing me on staff? At least as a fluffer. I could really do a ... Hello?"

Fuck.

Bastard.

CHAPTER FOUR

A LITTLE Bit About Me

I've had a modicum of success. *Modicum* is the type of success that forces you to remortgage your home, if you still have a home to remortgage, and utilize the two most important words in a writer's survival jargon: balance transfer. With credit card interest at a reasonable 92% it would be fiscally criminal not to take advantage of it. Even then there can be obstacles. The refinancing of our home was going along swimmingly, however since we rent I'd been dealing with what I thought is a petty and vindictive legal effort by my landlord to evict my family. Most financial experts I've spoken with have suggested that I might have to abandon my family to let them fend for themselves. My well-compensated *wife* refers to *modicum* as "the selfish, scum-sucking, piece of shit stipend that you try to pass off as a living wage."

My wife is my greatest advocate.

I've written for prime-time television constructing a lackluster career on the back of any friends who were in a position to hire me to write a script or, God willing, get me on staff.*[6]

Getting on staff brings about a hefty salary, healthy health benefits and calls returned from your agent. Dreams of long-term employment, a

---

6 *For those of you who are not showbiz savvy enough to understand the meaning of a staff hiring; Once a television show is approved to be the network's schedule, a staff, consisting of under forty-year-old, Jewish Ivy League graduates, an African American and a lesbian, is hired. If you can bring on an African American lesbian the Writers Guild you're permitted to hire one additional Jew.*

lifetime of residuals and syndication*⁷ are dashed immediately coinciding with the first network notes of the season.

Maybe if a whole bunch of successful comedy writers died, I'd be in a good position to get a job. In fact, I might even be able to have my own show.

One can dream.

Needing some type of revenue flow, I ended up writing for "Location, Location, Writing" – a showbiz monthly mag that focused two-thirds of its content on sight-scouting and a third on writing. They paid me for writing and, in a way, I was staying close to the industry just in case something popped.

And then I met Larry.

---

7 *After five years of airing shows, rights are sold to local and cable broadcasters for unrelenting replays of sitcoms that in many instances are not based on any reasonable thought processes. More information can be found in the success of the quintessential "King of Queens" phenomenon.*

CHAPTER FIVE

Larry[8]

For those who have been under a rock for the last twenty-five years, Larry is the genius behind *Seinfeld,* which if he did nothing else in his life it would have been enough to raise him to legend status. As Pricilla Pressley said, "You don't mess with perfection."

Seinfeld provided Larry and its star, Jerry Seinfeld, more money than you could donate to the United Jewish Appeal in a lifetime. He followed up with the HBO vunderseries, *Curb Your Enthusiasm*, for which he both wrote and starred.

Years before he became one of Hollywood's greatest business and romantic catches (his off-screen trysts are the stuff of small screen legend), Larry stalked the comedy club stages of Manhattan Island. Early in his career, many of his peers thought that his song parodies and jaunty prop humor would make him the next Gallagher (though Larry always saw himself as the next Bobo Brazil, a Shakespearian thespian in the 50s). Alas, unbeknownst to Larry, a deal with Satan had already been negotiated by twelve-year-old Scott Thompson who years later would turn the comedy world upside down with his brilliant satirical stylings under the nom deplume, Carrot Top.

8 *Mind you, this continues to be the fictional Larry David. I can't keep reminding you so please make a note to reference this information until you complete the book. Thank you.*

Larry was known as a comedian's comedian.*⁹ That meant that audiences had no idea what he was talking about and wondered aloud, mostly during his set, "how did this guy have the balls to think he was a comedian." In the old days they would say, "The guys in the band love him." Back then Larry would get reefer or a little Mary Jane from the band. If he ended up with reefer and Mary Jane, even better. Sometimes one of the older guys might invite Larry back to his place where he would ask Larry to, as they used to say, *blow their flugelhorn*. But in the comedy club world being a comedian's comedian comedian meant management usually put you on stage last. Still, Larry remained fairly optimistic, in a way that said, "suicide is an option, but not today."

To be sure there was no quit in Larry David. Oh sure, there were a lot of faking stomach aches and going home before his set, but never *quit*. He always felt that there was no place else to go but up. That was until rapid-fire, Boston-bred comic, Steven Wright, started working the club and was slotted next to last, making Larry even *laster*. Yes, Larry had been knocked down a notch, but nothing, not even the boos from his classic *Mother catching him masturbating during Shabbat* bit would stop him.

With that sense of vapid confidence, he packed his bags and was about to join a loose band of generic, gentile comics who were about to tour the Deep South comedy clubs, when at the last moment he was rescued by fellow Hebraic funny man, the cocksure Richard Lewis.

Known for his addiction to slimming, dark clothes, Lewis was another in a line of neurotic Jews who stalked the comedy club stage choosing not to waste their social anxiety on expensive therapists but instead cultivating them into material that would become a career path. He spoke in great detail of the comedy folklore, of a road to riches and manic-depressive Hollywood dreams fashioned by comics like Woody Allen, Robert Klein, and Albert Brooks (aka Albert Einstein, or whatever name Albert

9 *In truth, since the brilliant, young Gilbert Gottfried, whose best work would later come as an animatronic talking bird, was considered the New York comedy scene's comedian's comedian, Larry was in fact, the comedian's, comedian comedian.*

was using at the time so that people wouldn't know he was real smart or Jewish).

Larry was ready to follow Lewis westward.

Once landing on the L.A. scene, Larry's talent was immediately recognized, and was selected as a writer and featured performer on a sketch show I believe was called *Thursdays* that aired every Friday night. It was a sketch show's sketch show. Larry's performances would soon have *Thursdays'* audiences mention Larry in the me breath with the immortal half man, half chicken, half moyle, Lenny Schultz.

But New York continued to beckon for his return, the way a city beckons: silently, like a mime who refuses to be blown by the wind. Pizza in L.A., where Dominoes was considered a terrific neighborhood pizza joint, was inedible to Larry. He packed his material and a single portion of Ramon Noodles into a manila folder and returned to the Big Apple. *SNL*, the big boy on the block, discovered Larry was on his way back to New York and offered him a writing job.

The move did not exactly spell success. It barely spelled *suc*. Larry spent that season cultivating the one sketch of his that got onto the air. The inability of SNL producer, Lorne Michaels, to grasp the genius of Larry's wit was too much for Larry to bear. He wanted desperately to leave the show. Being that there was no quit in Larry and he would rather die than admit he had failed, he decided to fake a suicide by holding his breath during one of SNL's fifteen minute, one-joke sketches. With five minutes still remaining in the sketch, Larry passed out in one of John Belushi's dried up puke stains. Michaels replaced the frothing-from-the-mouth Larry with another Jew satisfying the mandatory ninety-two-Jewish-writers-per-sketch staff, Writers Guild minimum.

You know the one door closes and another opens thing? Well, it couldn't have been truer for Larry as his departure from *SNL* set the stage for his breakthrough film role as "Saul's friend" at the café in the Hank Jagger classic, *Rectum? I Nearly Killed Him*. I never saw the film but if you go to IMDB.com, the fine film reviewer from the blog, "Hi, I'm Troy and This Is My Blog," the inimitable troy-32, who had over 194 IMDB comments attributed to him, called *Rectum…* "unique."

For most of America though, Larry's story really began in 1989 when he and comedian Jerry Seinfeld co-created the show *Seinfeld* on NBC. People referred to it as "a show about lot of stuff but nothing you could put your finger on" which, in reality, was about vague indifference. But to this day, Larry refuses to specifically identify what that indifference was. Curiously, Larry is a leader in the struggle to get Carly Simon to reveal who was so vain.

With a cast including Julia Dreyfus (Elaine), Jason Alexander (George) and Michael Richards (Kramer), the show was not an immediate success. Speculation from those in the know was that this was due to audience's unfamiliarity with clever writing. Cultural researchers likened it to the shock a digestive system, accustomed to eating a daily ration of McDonald's burgers, feels the moment it is introduced to filet mignon. In the least there is some nausea and stomach discomfort associated with certain programming.

When the audience and their inflamed colons became accustomed to the smart writing along with the unique story lines, *Seinfeld* became the hit it deserved to be.[10]

The series provided Larry and Jerry with more money than needed to choke a horse, similar to the horse Kramer stuffed with flatulent-inducing kale, before kale was healthy. The type of success that *Seinfeld* begot is one or two of those exceptional feats that seem to slip by network programmers every ten years. In the '80s it was *The Simpsons* and *Cheers*. In the '70s, *All In The Family* and *M*A*S*H**. Before that, television was still in its infancy, its informative years, so everything was a risk and that in

---

10 *I ran into Jerry in the entry hall at L.A.'s Laugh Factory where I congratulated him on Seinfeld. He told me the show wouldn't last. I agreed and asked if I could submit a story idea before it was canceled. Haven't heard back.*

itself set up the conditions necessary to create some pretty special shows, sometimes twice in the same year.

1952: *I Love Lucy* and *Amos & Andy* gave screen time to a Latino and a bunch of *coloreds* before they could even use the same bathrooms as the white TV show characters.

1953: George Burns (breaking the 4th wall) and Gracie Allen, Jack Benny, Jackie Gleason and Milton Berle brought radio and vaudeville genius to the small screen.

1954: *Topper* and *Life of Riley*. Notso frightening ghosts and a regular fat guy.

1955: Red Skelton and Phil Silvers proved that variety wasn't dead.

Then again, TMZ (Too Much Zen) wasn't even a twinkle to Harvey Levin's eyes, so negative press was essentially nonexistent in the 50's: Liberace wasn't gay and Gale Storm was sober. On and on the early sitcoms made the funny. *Mayberry* and *Dobie Gillis* begat sidekick stars (Barney Fife and Maynard G). *Car 54, Where Are You, McHale's Navy* and *Hogan's Heroes* offered the obvious, but still funny side of uniformed work, World War II and the POW camps of the Third Reich.

The Dick Van Dyke Show should have shut down the sitcom industry forever due to the "You Can't Do Any Better So Why Try" rule, that has since been proven true some several hundred thousand times.

The last thirty or forty years, depending on the year you're reading this, the rule has been: one great sitcom every decade was acceptable, and for the stars and producers, no more than one great show a lifetime. Post-*Seinfeld*, Alexander and Richards adhered to the credo by refusing to risk a role that strayed even slightly from their *Seinfeld* characters or their shows themselves were more feeble than the characters they played. Only the adorable Dreyfus, achieved a success with the aid of her producer husband then wandered into premium cable land where she starred magnificently in *Veep* satirizing Vice President Tina Fey.

Seinfeld pretty much didn't even try, mostly limiting his appearances to standup or driving.

But Larry, Larry, Larry. Larry couldn't help himself. He thought he could stay under the radar. Forget network. He would try out one of them there new cable thingys. Larry took his creative genius and hard-to-conceal, leading man good looks to HBO and broke the rule. *Curb Your Enthusiasm*, Larry's homage to Larry, broke all the rules. It wasn't just another show about zilch. It was a show about even less. It didn't even have words, at least written ones. It was what Larry called "improvisational." Of course, Larry's improvisation never reached the lofty heights of a Wayne Brady, but since the presumed passing of the late, great David Spade, who has?

Larry explored every God-given neurosis known to Jew. Larry David, Larry David's character on *Curb...* made comedian Richard Lewis seem as stable as comedian Paul Reiser. Of course, some have said that Paul Reiser was Richard Lewis. Or was it the other way around? Actually, I've never seen either of them in the same room at the same time, though truth be told, I had once been in a room speaking to Lewis and from the corner of my eye I thought I saw Reiser at the door ready to walk into the room, but when I looked again he had disappeared.

While Larry thought he was only creating a new show, what he didn't understand was that he was also establishing a ripple that would quickly swell into a menacing tsunami leading to a tidal wave of defiance, climaxing with a mountainous valley of inappropriate metaphor.

And then there was... THE DANGER!

CHAPTER SIX

Interview Insolvency

Despite Larry's success, and perhaps because of it, didn't he have an obligation to share what had so benefited his own lot? How could he decide to pass on something that had already been planned for so long? He promised. Don't promises mean anything in Hollywood?*[11] What would one stinkin' hour out of his precious life hurt? I've been chasing that aberrant recluse for two fucking years and he can't give me one lousy hour?

What would I do now? I promised my editor the story. I told all my friends (friends who have been continually employed in the same business I am only allowed to sniff a few months a year) that I would be doing this extremely compelling interview. Now, not only don't I get the lousy five hundred dollars, but I won't be able to show my face at any studio-adjacent deli.

Okay. What's the fallback plan? I could tell everyone that my editor pulled the story. I certainly would have had no control over that, right? It's not like it hasn't happened before. Nah. Wouldn't pass muster with my so-very-employed friends. They'd wonder why I was no longer dropping my *I know Larry David* stories around every Fatburgers we'd meet at. Fatburgers, where I would slobber down greasy saturated fat while pissing on the business as I had always done following my interviews with legendary scribes like Larry Gelbart and Gary Marshall. Christ, Gelbart, who

---

11 *Promises in Hollywood, have always been the backbone of the business. Keeping them has been more the coccyx (the human tail bone that serves no purpose and is slowly vanishing).*

knew God and George Burns personally*[12], would do an interview with me but Larry D, wouldn't.

What a shit. He thinks he's so big. Yeah, well, did you ever see his movie, *Sour Grapes?*

Who am I kidding? Look at me. Could anyone be smaller? I love what the guy represents. His talent. His willingness to take risks. His height. Yet here I am ripping into him just to feel better about myself. Jealousy, the one motivating factor keeping me from drowning in a pool of my own self-pity.

Wait a minute. I'm a fucking writer. I should write about this. Not just an article or a column. I should write a book. A kind of unauthorized biography. And if no one will publish it, I'll publish it myself. You can do that now and make a bundle or so says the e-mail I got yesterday from WILLPUBANYSHIT.COM. In the least I can shoot it all over the Internet. Hell. I've already opened that Twitter account. Now I can do what it was meant to do: get my eight followers to viral my book.

I'll do it. I'll write "The Larry David Story," publish it myself and get it to all his friends. I'll get it to all the people he's turned down. Actually, I don't know if he's turned down anyone other than me but I'll make damn sure I get the book. Then I'll get it to all the guys who are still hanging out at the Improv and Comedy Store ten years after they sent in their AARP application. That'll do it. That'll give him his comeuppance.

I'll write the book, then the screenplay.

And I'll keep 100% of the dramatic rights.

I'd have to keep it under wraps, except of course for my editor who would be expecting the article. He knew how I felt about the unfairness of the writing business. I had joked to him that if only Larry, Matt Groening, Ricky Gervais, Seth MacFarlane, Chuck Lorre, James Brooks along with

---

12 *Do I really have to note that Gelbart wrote "Oh God" starring George Burns? Sorry. Nowadays, sadly, yes.*

a few thousand writers under the age of thirty committed suicide maybe then some show would hire me.

I meant it as a joke. It wasn't a very good joke. A little long-winded. As Leno told the silly-writing doctorate class I taught at Temple University in Philadelphia, "Use the fewest number of words to a punchline." I'll try it out Monday at The Comedy Store, that is if Andrew Dice Clay doesn't come in and bump me into Tuesday morning with the same crap he's been doing for thirty years.

Of course, it's going to be a little tricky. Everyone else I know will tell me I shouldn't do it. The same way they said it was a bad idea when I tried to sell Steven Spielberg's family on eBay without his authorization. As if he would have given me the okay. They'd tell me that I'd never work in this town again. Hah. My favorite threat: *People who aren't hiring me, won't hire me.* What a risk.

Let's see. Where do I start? I have to keep it fair, balanced and literate. Not a hint of vindictiveness. After the book sells gangbusters, people (studios) need to see this as a vehicle they can easily star-cast.

I remember hearing how difficult it was to cast *Wired,* the John Belushi biopic. No one would touch it. Belushi, a darling of the industry had died after years of being an out of control, obsessive-compulsive drug addict. Making a movie that revealed him to be an out of control, obsessive-compulsive, drug addict was too offensive to the industry and would have made it much harder for the Chris Farleys of the world to tap into the wonderful world of excess that John had discovered. If anyone would allow himself to be casted as Belushi, his career would be dead. Dead, you hear!

They ended up casting some unknown by the name of Michael Chiklis. Did this guy ever work again? Okay, he did, but not for a few years. 'Course he only ended up copping a Golden Globe and an Emmy for a fucking USA Network show.

If I write a decent screenplay, there'll be a flood of Michael Chiklises*[13] begging to audition. But if I was going to write something that puts my heart on the line, I'd need to do it right. I needed to speak to someone who wasn't afraid to take risks… real risks… literary risks. The type of risk that a writer takes when he/she invests his/her credibility and his/her time into creating something/somewhat so original no one could say for sure whether it would draw an audience. Or in some cases, writing something so innovative that an audience would understand what the writer/writress is trying to say. In effect, risking career and livelihood.

And so it was, my friends, that there was only one writer in Hollywood who had shown that he feared nothing, at least on a literary basis.

I needed to get some advice from the best.

---

13 *What kind of name is Chiklis anyway? No wonder he didn't work for such a long time. You can't count "Fantastic Four." Hulk's makeup could have been applied to Julia Roberts and it would have worked. Christ. Didn't his management have a clue?*

CHAPTER SEVEN

Getting Back to Getting Back at Larry

It wouldn't be easy. If I was going to write a book on Larry David I'd first have to study him, his every move, his diet, his purging, his lack of dieting, his clothing and how in the world his shirts became all the rage. I'd have to know his likes and dislikes, crawl inside his skin and feel what he feels, think what he thinks. And when I crawled inside him I'd have to make sure that I kept his thoughts and his feelings separate from my own so that I wouldn't get confused, rethinking and re-feeling*14 my own thoughts. Would that be possible? I could only try.

I set out to find Larry. I had seen *Curb Your Enthusiasm* enough to know what Larry's house looked like, but getting there was the problem. I GPS'd "Larry's House" but ended up at the Larry the Cable Guy's mansion that he paid for with "git 'er done" chits. Git 'er done. It's so G-d damn funny every time I hear it. Here's a tip. When you come up with a good catchphrase, drill it into the fucking ground, through every single layer of earth until you hit China. Then find out how to say it in Chinese and start drilling it into their skulls. Remember not to bypass Australia. You just cannot use it too much.

---

14 . *So, why is "rethinking" one word and "re-feeling" needs to be hyphenated? You have to ask why "no one" is two words and "nobody" is one word? Answer: Welcome to the English language. To be clear, the American English language as opposed to the bastard, colony-pursuing United Kingdom English language.*

I headed down to Sunset to meet with my undercover celebrity map guy. I slipped him a sawbuck, one of those new ones where you could actually see President Saw's eyes twinkle.

I followed the map's directions to an inconspicuous mansion sitting in the middle of a drive through cul de sac. If not for the fifty-foot hedges sculpted into the shapes of some of the many of Larry's top neuroses I might have missed the house altogether: Shame and Paranoia – with Guilt and Compassion conspicuously missing – flanking each side of the massive front doors.

On Larry's front step was a stack of old People Magazines. I had heard of Larry's incessant desire to keep tabs on the lives of the hottest stars while hoping that one day fans would be keeping tabs on him. Even as a child he had dreamt of paparazzi following his every move. So much was his desire for others to think he was popular in middle school he paid his best friend, Esther Thinsthith, to follow him around with one of those cardboard cameras that they made in elementary school. Just to make sure that kids took notice, he would humiliate Esther by calling her "star-fucker" in front of the lunch ladies, when in fact, Esther had never fucked a real star (despite the uproarious success of "Son-in-law," Pauly Shore was never considered a star) though she did know Pauly in a biblical sense.

During *Seinfeld* when the publicity efforts didn't attract the quality rags Larry rehired Esther who he ended up firing again because she was receiving more publicity than he. The former stalker now has her own magazine, "Watch Out, She's in The Bushes," which follows the every move of today's hottest stalkers.

I picked up one of the magazines and walked towards the door. I hoped that my magazine-delivery boy ruse might get me through the master's portals and I would soon meet the man who had changed television. Not as big a change as when they started to play commercials louder than regular programming, but still, a change for the better.

I approached the door, swallowing hard, unsuccessfully attempting to persuade the ever-present glob of anxiety-generated saliva that seemed to have taken up permanent residence in my throat to dislodge and move down into wherever it's supposed to go next. With a deep breath that seemed to carry a toxic mixture of excitement and anxiety, I raised my hand to knock. But before my fist reached the door, the door opened.

To my complete surprise, there stood Michael Richards (Seinfeld's Kramer). He wore a tuxedo much like a butler or a penguin who worked as a butler, might. I was surprised, to say the least, that he did not do one of those Kramer-like door-fall-ins (which got old real fast on Seinfeld though it did not stop Larry from choreographing it into every fucking episode).

"Yes?"

"I, um, I'm here for Mr. David's People Magazine interview."

I handed him my card.

He checked out the card. "You write AND do stereo repair?"

"It's kind of a joke."

"Well, I'm not sure whether the boss will be seeing anyone."

He closed the door. What the hell was that all about? Richards is working for Larry as his butler? The guy won three Emmys. Talk about come downs.

After about five minutes, Richards not returning, I raised my hand to knock again.

CHAPTER EIGHT

Hello Larry

(Apologies to the Late, Great McLean Stevenson)

As if I had just become Curly (it could have been Shemp, but definitely not Curly Joe who ended up on Abbott and Costello's show, which I believe was called *The Abbott and Costello Show*), I ended up knocking on Larry David's head.

Yes, thee Larry David. My Larry David.

"Yes?"

His voice was just like it was on television, on *Curb Your Enthusiasm,* though not much like when he voiced over the back of the head of, I don't know, New York Knicks owner, James Dolan, on *Seinfeld* (could have been George Steinbrenner).

It was years later when I learned that the person sitting in the chair was the back of some actor they paid to play the part. Of course, it could have been one of the writers on staff. It was nice that Larry would throw his writers a bone by letting them appear on screen (Bob Shaw and Carol Leifer among others)

"*People Magazine* delivery boy." I disguised my voice with a deep base tone that was more reminiscent of a woman trying to sound like a man.

"There's no delivery boy for *People*. It comes through the mail."

Was he on to me?

"Did I say delivery boy? I meant, reporter."

"Where's your camera? *People* never does a story without plenty of pictures."

He was right. *People* was a classy literary gazette, but its trademark was the photos of the hot stars. No real *People* journalist would go anywhere without a camera.

Thinking fast, I pulled out my cell phone.

"We do it all by phone now."

I waited a heart-skipping beat as I watched Larry deliver his patented squint of suspicion which soon turned into a smile of acceptance. Holy crap! Mr. Rodgers was right, God rest his soul. A smile is a frown turned upside down.

"Yeah. Alright. Come on in."

Score!

I went to shake his hand. He stepped back, his grimace shot lazar-like though my retinas.

"I… I don't shake," said Larry.

"Got it."

"Don't touch anything," he said as he turned to walk into his house.

As I followed Larry in, all I could keep thinking was, what a great ass. I mean, for a man of his age. I had been a long time heterosexual and plan to stay that way, but there is no denying, a great ass is a great ass. Of course, it was covered by pants, which we should know is no true indication of the actual ass's appearance… thank God.

Clothes are the great and worthy deceivers. They cover, lift, separate and distort delivering a false, perfected image of what lay beneath the material. Similar to a good brassiere you're really guessing what lies behind. This isn't to say that they don't have a noble purpose. Once revealed, what might have been thought to be unaffected by aging gravity and loosening gluteus muscles, now presents the truth in all its sagging and wrinkled honesty. Since we only get to see the completely exposed derrieres of such a small percentage of those we pass on a daily basis, why would we not want the most perfected imagery well-designed clothing provides?

Larry led me past his foyer filled with elegantly framed copies of every residual check he ever received. There was no hint of ego though there was an obvious desire to show people who walked into his house that he had made more money and gained more success than they had.

Below each check was a photo-shopped nude*15 picture of every woman Jerry had *dated* on *Seinfeld*.

While *Seinfeld* was at its height and Jerry was dating large-breasted teens to get the attention of his peer comics, Larry had a bit of jealous admiration. To compensate he coerced every woman he dated under a 36C to get breast implants that had been donated by parents of recently deceased Dallas Cowboy cheerleaders who had been booked as stunt doubles. These peppy young gals had all died in a rather suspicious accidents on the *Seinfeld* set where they had been casted as stand-ins for Elaine's abominable hip-hop dance scene. The dance caused a high number of back spasms for Dreyfus and her doubles, though curiously, only Dreyfus survived the spasms. The doubles died from a lack of adequate treatment on the set and once the mass mastectomies were performed the cadavers were all transferred over to the ABC Family network*16 where no one noticed the bodies… nor the shows.

We sat in the living room where I couldn't take my eyes off the portrait above the fireplace. It was the one of Kramer, made famous during the episode in which an elderly couple purchased a painting of Kramer

15 *While no female character actually appeared in the nude on the show, there was one female character on the show who was assumed to be nude during filming, but she was actually played by Larry who was dressed in a female nude costume.*

16 *Later rebranded to Freeform, a sub-division of the Disney Entertainment.*

for $5,000. But in this painting, in place of Kramer's face, was Larry's. Nice touch.

"Before we do this, I need you to sign these," said Larry.

Larry presented a couple of litigious-looking documents with everything covered other than spaces where he wanted me to sign.

"What are these?" I asked.

"Standard interview agreements. You know, making sure that you only use what we speak about for your article. Someone in my position needs to protect himself from being exploited."

"I… I wouldn't ever do anything that would harm you or your reputation."

"Yeah. Sure. That's why you'll sign these. Of course, if you don't want the interview…"

"No, no, no. I'll sign them. Where do I sign?"

Larry pointed to the signature blocks.

"Can I read it first?"

"So, you don't want to do the interview…"

He started to get up.

"No! Let me have those."

He laid them on the coffee table and I signed. Makes sense. Really, he was Larry David.

He folded them up and tucked them in his pocket.

"Can I get a copy?"

"You have a copy machine with you?"

"I don't normally carry…"

"So, how do we do this?" interrupted Larry. "What do you want to know?"

Wow. Here I was ready to crawl inside his head and sponge up all the dirt from a show biz deity. I now had the opportunity to do the interview I originally wanted to do.

"I didn't think you did interviews," I said. "At least that's what you told a friend of mine who is not me."

"I usually don't. But, come on ... *People*."

He had me there.

"Um. Why do you think there's so much crap on TV?"

Suddenly the smile on his face turned upside down into a frown.

Holy moley. It works both ways.

Larry seemed buried in thought as if his answer would come from deep within his soul but was abruptly interrupted by the ringing from the ESPN football helmet phone next to him. Larry picked it up without as much as a "hello." He listened for a couple brief seconds, hung up and then, without another word, his face filled with sadness. He stood and walked out of the room.

I sat there wondering what had happened. I knew that at Larry's age, prostrate problems and Lilliputian kidneys, led to a lot of quick exits. Still, even the most elderly, no matter their state of senility, didn't need a phone call to remind them to urinate.

Richards appeared.

"Mr. David asked me to show you the door," his voice jumped back and forth between his Kramer character and Edward Everett Horton[17] on the movie-butler scale. If it weren't that I had written it myself I would have said Richards was being a tad bit bi-butler.

"Is this a joke?" I asked.

"The boss don't do no jokin'," said Richards.

17 *Since E.E. Horton died quite a bit ago, you can familiarize yourselves with his credits that made him the preeminent film butler for decades at http://www.imdb.com/name/nm0002143/ as well as the narrator for Fractured Fairy Tales on "Rocky and His Friends."*

"What?" which was the least of hundreds of questions swirling in my head.

"The boss doesn't write jokes. He gets his laughs from the situations that his characters deal with."

"How are you a butler?"

He leaned in and whispered.

"I take what I can get. Did you see my last set at the Laugh Sweatshop?"

I had seen the cell phone video on TMZ and thought it best to drop it.

"When can I talk with him again?"

"The boss won't be giving any more interviews."

I noticed a shimmer swell in Richard's eyes. A hint of a tear. Grief had fallen over the David household. I shook my head and walked out. Just moments before I had wanted to write a homily ripping Larry a new asshole and now I actually felt a twinge of sadness for the guy. Damnit. Seems, at least for Larry, success did not equal contentment.

Then it hit me.

I felt like such a shit. It wasn't Larry who was the asshole. It was me. I was loading up all my resentment from a personal lack of success at his feet. Here I was thinking that even though he didn't know me at all, he was the symbol of my discontent. I should have just thanked Larry for even considering doing the interview and left it at that. I loathed myself, which was nothing new but at least, this time, I had a valid reason.

I sat in my car, replaying the conversation again and again. What happened? What did I say that could have upset Larry so much? What was the capital of New Hampshire? The questions swirled in my cerebral cortex, questions that might never be answered. Untold ramifications abounded not the least was the question: if no one knew the capital of New Hampshire where would the legislature go to legislate? Then there're the early primaries.

Pow!

A gun shot?!

I cautiously snuck around to the back of the house where Richards whisked past me.

I moved to the window and what I saw sent a shock through my entire body. In a large opulent bedroom was a blood-spattered Larry David, eyes rolled back into his blood-soaked skull.

As I wrote somewhere around page twelve, something was wrong.

CHAPTER EIGHT

Goodbye Larry

I guardedly entered the house through the door Richards had left flung open and walked into the bedroom. Actually, I had stumbled in half-expecting the studio audience, had there been one, to roar in acknowledgment hoping that it was Kramer stumbling through the doorway again.

I stood there a moment, half-trying not to throw up and half-salivating over the fact that I was staring at one of the biggest show biz stories since Bob Crane killed Sal Mineo.*[18]

There laid Larry David, naked from the waist up, arms at his side, soft-uncalloused fingers resting atop his opposing hand's fingers. He was posed bizarrely similar to Kramer had in the afore mentioned portrait. Odd. Coincidence, I was sure. Still, odd.

Under his hand was a business card. Looking closer… it was MY card. Great, my timing is always impeccable. Years of relentless networking attempting to be known to those in power. Had not the gods grasped my intention to connect with those still alive?

I noticed blood-soaked script pages crumpled up just under Larry's other hand. Pulling them gently from his hand I slowly read, quietly

---

18 *Both Crane and Mineo were murdered. Who's to say who murdered whom and it won't be settled by this tome as in the next edition, Mineo will be accused of murdering Crane. If I would be so fortunate as to have a third edition or even a paperback, I hope I'll be able to announce both actors are still alive.*

attempting to pay some sort of reverence to what might have been the last piece of work created by the genius of Larry David.

SEINFELD

"THE CONSPIRACY"

TEASER

FADE IN:

EXT. MANHATTAN CORNER – DAY

KRAMER STANDS ON SOAP BOX IN THE MIDDLE OF A BUSY INTERSECTION. PASSERBYS IGNORE HIM.

KRAMER

Je mendie de vous. Etre jamais vigilant comme vous tentez de faire quelque sens de l'extraordinaire. Pour pendant que votre quête peut être honorable, les réponses que vous découvrez déchireront de côté chaque brin seul de ce que vous avez cru pour avoir raison avec le monde. Quel était une fois une vérité simple, existe uniquement pour cacher une fosse sans fond de devinettes de unrelenting; un labyrinthe si complexe a fait pour étouffer la vie de solution prête; révélant des conspirations si sombre, donc refroidir, donc extraordinairement complexe la subversion, beaucoup d'entre ceuxlà qui a été profondément complice dans le terrain, ne pas avoir d'idée qu'ils étaient. ..complicit.

(TRANSLATION: I beg of you. Be ever vigilant as you attempt to make some sense of the extraordinary. For while your quest may be honorable, the answers you discover will tear apart every single shred of what you believed to be right with the world. What was once a simple truth, solely existed to cloak a bottomless pit of unrelenting riddles; a labyrinth so complete, crafted to choke the life out of any ready solution; revealing conspiracies so dark, so chilling, so extraordinarily complex, the subversion that so many of those

who have been deeply complicit in the plot, had no idea that they were ... complicit.)

PASSERBY

I love the French. They're so down-to-earth.

KRAMER

Les prises d'énigme dans lui une réponse ; et la réponse tient dans elle la vérité de la toute la vie.

(Translation: The riddle holds within it an answer; the answer holds all life's truths.)

JERRY AND GEORGE WALK UP TO KRAMER.

JERRY

Kramer. What are you doing?

KRAMER

Hey, Jerry. Is America great or what? I get to speak my mind and not have to worry about being arrested for treason, or worse, public nudity.

JERRY

But you're not nude.

KRAMER

Only to those who fear to look deeper, mon Jer. Underneath these clothes, I am completely buck au natural. Commando, Jerry!

GEORGE

When did you learn how to speak French?

KRAMER

I didn't. But they don't know that. Sounds pretty sexy, huh? It's the language of love, and above all, I am a lover.

GEORGE

Above all, you're nuts.

KRAMER

Only on the surface. One must look within to find one's true self.

JERRY

Has your "true self" been smoking something?

KRAMER

Only the truth, Jerry. Only the truth. I've been swallowing the man's lies for way too long. I have seen the Promised Land and...

GEORGE

Yep. He's been smoking.

JERRY

We're going to get something to eat. Wanna come?

GEORGE

He's gotta have the munchies.

KRAMER

Can't right now, mon cheri. You see, I have a dream that one day we will not be judged by the color of our skin but by the content of our character.

GEORGE

And now he's black.

KRAMER

I have seen the Promised Land. Now I may not get there with you…

JERRY

Let's go. I've got a French toast jones bad.

JERRY AND GEORGE WALK OFF.

GEORGE

Why do they call it French toast? Really, it has nothing to do with France. It's not toasted. It's soaked in eggs and pan fried.

JERRY

You couldn't toast it. The eggs would slip off.

KRAMER

I have a dream today that when we let freedom ring; we let it ring from every village and every hamlet, from every state and every city, so that all of God's children, black men and white men, Jews and Gentiles, Muslims and those who are forced to live in Ohio, will be able to join hands and sing in the words of the old Negro spiritual, "Free at last! Free at last! Thank God Almighty, we are free at last!" Les prises d'énigme dans lui une réponse; et la réponse tient dans elle la vérité de la toute la vie.

(Translation: The riddle holds in it an answer; and the answer holds within it the truth of all life.)

PASSERBY

I love the French. They're so down-to-earth.

FADE OUT

END OF SHOW

Huh? What a piece of crap. It wasn't funny at all. My sample*[19] *Seinfeld* was far funnier and although not one agent, producer or network executive agreed, you have to be the type of person who believes in yourself. You must be able to say, "they just don't get me" or "they don't know quality"… or "fuck it."

'Course, his script page could have been a first draft. Muriel Hemingway always said that her grandfather – I forget his name right now – said that "the first draft of anything is shit." Yeah, that's it – it was a first draft. Or could it be some sort of… oh, my God… suicide note?

I took a step back. What was I missing? Something in the script? His Kramer-like pose? Then again, what was the crimson-colored fish lying next to his feet all about? Upon closer inspection it was not just any fish. It was a herring. A red-herring.*[20] Maybe these were all red-herrings, even the ones that weren't red nor herringish, so to speak.

What about the blood-inscribed pentacle on his stomach?

BLOOD-INSCRIBED PENTACLE ON HIS STOMACH?!

How in the world did I miss that?

Wait. It wasn't a pentacle at all. Instead of a five-point star within a circle, the star had six points. A Jewish star. A Star of David.

Omigod!!!

Larry David was Jewish?

That's when my thoughts were interrupted by the need to survive, number one on the top five needs on Time Magazine's *Keys to Survive* list. Luckily, I could tell the gumshoes what happened, at least as much as I

---

19 *Television writers create sample scripts of existing programs to show agents, producers and network executives how well they can write those types of shows. My Seinfeld went to all History Channel showrunners.*

20 *A technique of training hounds to follow a scent, or of distracting hounds during a fox hunt, but modern linguistic research suggests that it was most likely a literary device invented in 1807 by English polemicist William Cobbett, and never an actual practice of a hunter (Wikipedia).*

knew. It wasn't like I was a witness to the actual shooting or that I had a motive.

Hmm.

Oh… shit.

As I jumped the hedges into the yard next door I was moving as fast as fact could move, still stuffing the evidence, er, um, script into my pocket. I was hoping there would be no proof that I had been there. Sure, the car that I owned and abandoned in the driveway might indicate to some that I could have been at the scene. Maybe the fact that my business card was still at the scene.

D'oh.

Still, it's not like the police wouldn't give me the benefit of the doubt. I'm a comedy writer. Comedy writers don't kill. It's comedians who do. Y'know, except for the ones who don't, but the next day on Facebook they write that they did.

CHAPTER NINE

Too Funny, Too Fat

Down a piece on Sunset Boulevard in the same Chateau Marmont bungalow where John Belushi decided to set in motion a *Belushi to Candy to Farley* series of *comedy ain't all that funny when you're a fat corpse* death, our camera sweeps through a bathroom door. Inside we find the former Hollywood power broker and now shamed-draped, Michael Ztivo, eating a bag of Chicken McNuggets while seated on an extra-wide, specially elevated toilet.

A single McNugget slipped from his tiny fingers and splashed into the crowded toilet water. Without missing a beat, Ztivo reached into the water and fished out the soggy tidbit. After dripping honey barbeque sauce from a small packet onto the Mcthingy, he dropped it into his mouth, whole.

Ztivo was once the widely feared kingmaker from Coldhearted Arrogant Assassins (CAA), the agency that launched an entertainment empire built on the backs of diabolic deals, stolen clients and solid-gold parachutes. But bad business deals and *Fuck me? Fuck you!* retribution replaced his once lavish control of tinsel town with a sad autobiographical story of a broken man.

Michael Ztivo was the definition of show biz clout with a presence so large that it demanded at least three strategically-placed tables at the former hot-spot Mortons, located at Melrose and Robertson, even when he was eating at The Ivy, three blocks away. His fall from omnipotence left a black hole nearly wide enough to accommodate his entire ego.

What does a man do when he faces adversity, a terrible loss, a failure of body and soul?

The answer is obvious: blame everyone else. And do it publicly ... in every possible way: social media, anti-social media, TV, radio, press, pony express and airplanes towing messages across the skies over east and west coast beaches.

After a sufficient number of flushes, Ztivo plodded from the bathroom to his well-worn, sheet-less twin mattress. Once seated, he pulled down his frayed, but expensive Armani slacks, baggy enough to hide at least three pilfered ICM clients. He placed a sharply spiked Versaci belt around his pale white, but sufficiently-hairy thigh, tightening it so that it cut into his thick flesh. Yet instead of writhing in what should have been intense pain, a serene smile, signaling that all was right with the world, crossed his lips.

Ztivo had buried as many a career as he had created. His debt to those he offended was overflowing, yet he felt no responsibility to right his wrongs. Instead, he found that purging his sins by pursuing deeper, more vicious sins, was giving him more satisfaction than the deeds he'd carried out in years past as the entertainment antichrist.

Picking up his cell phone he hit Auto-1.

"It's done," announced Ztivo, a hint of his old self-confidence reemerging.

"And they think we know not what we do," the voice exclaimed. "How they mock us."

"As they have mocked my innate right to threaten the life and career of every pathetic two-bit actor, writer or director," replied a grinning Ztivo.

"You have done a great service to G/god," said the voice not clear as to whether he was speaking of a higher power the word "G/god" necessitated a capital *G* or not. Nor was there any consideration as to whether there was a preference for God over G-d, or visa-versa. It's as confusing as the previous sentence.

Despite our leaders speaking of uniting the people, spelling has never been as divisive as it is today. Though many immigrants fled the spelling-intolerant old country to settle in a new land where those of different spelling and grammar belief systems could live side by side with those who might choose to use better or gooder grammar. Though many will point to how the Founders conjugated and believed that grammar was not a living model for expressing oneself, there is absolutely no mention of spelling in either the Constitution or Federalist papers. Only in James Madison's notes is there any reference to the proper use of homonyms yet in doing so he misused the word "ewe" when plainly the proper word should have been "you."

"We have waited centuries for this," said the voice on the other end.

"Thank you, Master."

Ztivo hung up the phone, proud of his work. His purpose was chaste. Doing God's work, fighting a virtuous war against the opponents of what you believe to be just, absolves one from responsibility for the means and methods wielded to attain victory. So it is written… somewhere.

Absolution requires sacrifice. For Ztivo, it meant the sacrifice of others.

He stood, shaking with delight, letting the sheer joy of his accomplishments cascade over him. Finally, he spoke to himself.

"Man, I am good."

Pulling close the heroin-soaked drapes once snorted by Jim Morrison during his penning of "People Are Strange," Ztivo stripped naked and knelt in the center of his room. Looking down, he examined the spiked Versaci belt clamped around his thigh. All true followers of *The Purpose* used the serrated binding to gouge the skin as reminder of The Masters' suffering.

The joyous pain also replaced masturbation as an obsession so manifest that the zealous recruitment of Catholic boys in *le order* was made unnecessary though it caused the secret handshake to be disregarded.

It is written, though difficult to read, as those pages are stuck together.

Grasping the buckle, Ztivo drew it one notch tighter, wincing as the needle-thin spikes dug deeper. Gasping with delight, he treasured his doctrinal absolution.

"Pain is good. Quality is overrated," he whispered, repeating the sacred mantra of Arthur Godfrey – the *Host of all Hosts*. Although Godfrey died in 1983, his amateur talent television show, *Talent Scouts*, was the forerunner of reality shows to come, filling valuable broadcast time by using cheap and inexperienced talent. His message continues to reverberate. Behind the curtains the many lackey programmers who followed Godfrey had performed the sacred practice known as *l'hémorrhagie du public* (bleeding the public dry).

Ztivo whispered a solemn prayer.

"Pouvoir mon sang et le sang de ces agents qui est allé avant que me suis ait nettoyé de tout sens de culpabilité." ("*May my blood and the blood of those agents who have gone before me be cleansed of all sense of culpability.*")

He once more tightened the sharpened, yet fashionable sartorial belt.

"Pouvoir mon sang et le sang de ces agents qui est allé avant que me suis ait nettoyé de tout sens de culpabilité." (Geez. Translated a couple lines above)

Again, as if an ex-Olympic swimmer, twenty years past competition weight, attempting to squeeze into his old bathing briefs, Ztivo pulled mightily to reach the last straining belt-loop.

"Pouvoir mon sang et le sang de ces agents qui est allé avant que me suis ait nettoyé de tout sens de culpabilité."

Finally, he felt the blood begin to flow. He was once again at peace.

CHAPTER TEN

On The Run

I sat in a cheap, south of Ventura Boulevard (Van Nuys adjacent) motel room, feeling more like a skid row David Janssen (or Harrison Ford, depending on whether you choose to make this a television or a film reference to *The Fugitive*) then a barely over the age of staff-consent, comedy writer. I couldn't go back to my home. If I knew those crack Beverly Hills detectives, they would have already dusted my car for prints. I always wore my Costco, bona fide faux, squirrel fur, driving gloves for just such an occasion. I'd be free and clear if not for the registration card that sat innocently in the glove compartment screaming silently my name, address and presumed guilt.

Police would probably be swarming my house by now. I tried to call my wife to explain, but the phone was busy. Damn. I should have ordered that fancy call-waiting feature everyone was talking about a few years back.

The Larry David (gasp) murder would be all over the TV. There would be some who would say it was suicide, but no one who knew him would buy Larry having the guts to kill himself. He barely allowed himself to have sex because of the genital discomfort he felt just toward the conclusion of his orgasm. Anyway, why would he? He had more money and success than he could have ever dreamed. No matter how neurotic one might believe Larry to be, the one thing friends would swear to, keeping in mind I was not one of those friends, was that Larry David was too selfish to leave all that to someone else.

There I go again, besmirching Larry to make me feel better about myself. I'm sure Larry wasn't too selfish to kill himself. It's just that suicide by repeated bludgeoning is one of the least preferred suicide methods according to "Suicide Quarterly," the bible of self-destruction.

The pundits would be filling the cable news networks, 24/7, speculating as to who might want Larry dead. But while he was not a beloved figure in terms of say, *I Love Lucy*'s William Fraley*[21], he just wasn't the type of guy who would engender a passion for his murder from friend or enemy. Sure, he might be left off Christmas card lists, but murder? I think that would be considered overkill.

Murder/overkill. See what I did there? Reminds me that I am somewhat of a word wrangler who's not afraid to craft homicidal wit.

Kewl.

Could he have been involved in some sordid affair that a distraught husband or boyfriend found out about? Like I said, Larry was truly flabbergasted by his run of inconceivable luck, including sex with gorgeous women who were willing to endure all of his maddening idiosyncrasies. He would have had to been stupid to blow that. Larry was a lot of things – actually not so many – but one of the things he wasn't, was stupid.

Perhaps a business deal gone sour? But Larry no longer had to make business deals or venture capital investments. Why would he? He didn't have to risk his own money. Networks were tripping over one another just for the possibility that he would let them pour money over his slim but wiry body. The only way he could die from business is if he suffocated under all his cash. There weren't enough banks in the country to handle all the deposits. In fact, to make the banks' job all the more difficult Larry's contracts called for payments to be made in silver dollars. Banks had to stay open late just to count his residuals.

---

21 *I hesitate to place a wink and a nod footnote as anyone who has some semblance to television history know of the general dislike of William Fraley by other cast members. Of course, it was only a hesitation as you can read here, I don't trust the majority of readers to grasp the sarcasm. Then again, really, who reads footnotes besides you?*

Of course, the investigators would have to take a good look at his relationships. That would probably go nowhere as Larry had every woman he dated, even a one night stand, sign a prenup which required her to die before him. No woman he knew intimately could have killed him. They were all legally bound not to. If they did, they wouldn't get a thing.

Could it have been an irate fan taking out his or her dissatisfaction with Larry's work? Not likely. Larry's shows only drew adoring fans. And if they weren't fans they wouldn't be able to tell Larry David from Jim Marshall, the former Minnesota Viking star defensive lineman and member of the famed Purple People Eater defense who once picked up a fumble and ran the wrong way ending up scoring for the other team in a 1962 National Football League game against the San Francisco 49ers.*[22]

I turned on the NBC's junior varsity's network, MSNBC, but found that the network had replaced its morning programming with a test pattern that was pulling in a better share than *Morning Joe*.

I checked evening programming to find out what the wily Chris Matthews (he was there then) would say – the word on the street was that Matthews was a closet Larry David addict. I was sure that Chris would make the passing of Larry the main subject of his show. I watched and while he may have spoken about Larry, with Chris talking over every one of the guests I couldn't understand what anyone was talking about. Fact is, Chris had brilliantly crafted a skill where he not only incessantly talked over every guest, but he could also speak over himself, therefore making it impossible for Chris to know for sure what he himself was saying.

22 *Though thoroughly humiliated, Marshall came out in the second half and played the best half of his life including forcing the fumble with which NFL Hall of Fame teammate, Alan Page, picked up and scored the winning touchdown. (You could read more from Jim's own mouth in my book, "Great Failures of the Extremely Successful, Mistakes, Adversity, Failure and Other Steppingstones to Success" www.greatfailure.com). I'm not sure if anyone has ever promoted their nonfiction book in their fiction book, but I'll check Amazon a couple weeks after this gets published and see when it was a smart move or seriously embarrassing.*

I flipped through the free *networks* which meant that I had to sift through the *elite liberal* spin to determine the truth of the news. Damn you, Al Roker! Christ, you might as well just write for Pravda.

NBC had yet to completely fill the wingtips of the venerable Tom Brokaw, with every fill-in attempt so inept allowing the news on Larry to slip by.

I switched to ABC, but the fill-in anchor, an actual boat anchor (animated, of course), was *reporting* on same ole, same ole wolverine shortage in the British Honduras. By this time, you would think the Hondurans would have moved to more wolverine-thriving locales.

Finally, and much to my chagrin, I had to turn on CBS and new anchor, Dane Cook, a socialist so thick she made Saul Alinsky sound like Pat Robertson, but without the southern drawl. Not really. Saul could no more be mistaken for Pat Robertson than wolverines would suddenly begin to thrive in the British Honduras.

I flicked on the radio turning quickly past NPR so as to not be taken in, nay hypnotized, by their incessant begging for funds. Isn't it enough that I donated that one year to what used to be Jerry's Kids? I tried every radio station, including all five thousand that carried Sean Hannity, and still, nothing.

I just didn't understand. It had been hours since I found Larry's body and the police should have already sent in their preliminary reports. Why wasn't his death being reported, and if it wasn't, could it also be that they hadn't thought to check me out?

I called my house and this time, instead of a busy signal, I was greeted by the brand new computer-generated (CG) phone company voice, so ingeniously irritating, that many callers who misdialed or called a non-working number, would then go to most any length not to use any phone device again perchance they will have to hear the grating CG voice once more.

Able to hang on just long enough to get the gist of message, I was told that I had dialed a non-working number. Odd. I knew my own number pretty well and other than the drunk I threw the night I was hired on staff of the show, *For Crissakes* (a religious comedy so bad that it was canceled before the first script had been written), I had never misdialed before.

This time, fingering the phone digits carefully lest I had to confront *The Voice*, I dialed and was greeted by another voice, this one not as irritating, but even more disconcerting.

"The number you dialed was dialed correctly but is not a working number. In fact, it never has been operational."

Drat.

CHAPTER ELEVEN

Something Smells Like H: HBO

I woke up with a hangover though I hadn't had a drop of alcohol the night before. Wait a minute. Does 100 proof Southern Comfort have alcohol in it? Okay, one bottle, but still, the hangover was more dread-driven than alcoholic residue (I have to remember to use that at my next AA networking meeting. Sounds humble. Gets a terrific reaction.).

Was yesterday a dream? A nightmare bred out of my lack of career success?

I wiped away the cobwebs with some cold java I found at the bottom of a Starbuck's cup someone had left under the radiator and reached out the door for my complimentary copy of *USA Today*. After I was through marveling at the outstanding color presentation of international weather, I went from front page to last, only stopping to find out what the late Larry King had to say about the misunderstood talents of Khloe Kardashian. Really. She has so much to give and people only focus on is her lactose intolerance. It just isn't fair.

But… not even an obituary reference to Larry's passing.

I turned on *The Today Show*. I hadn't watched it since Katie Couric was replaced by someone who's since been replaced by someone who has also been replaced. Whomever she was she was quite sweet and enthusiastic, but no one wakes up a man's innards quite the way cutacious Katie did. If truth be known, many an intimate evening spent with my darling wife was sustained due to thoughts of Katie. Unfortunately, while Katie's perkiness perked me up, many were the times they had saddled her with a hairstyle clearly exposing her entire forehead.

What were they thinking?

I stayed tuned long enough for the headlines, bereft of any mention of Larry's death. Then, as I was about to switch from *The Today Show* to *Fox and Friends* (the nation's news program of record), they teased a guest spot with Sarah Jessica Parker who would be promoting the next big *Sex and the City* reunion. I was never an *SATC* fan. To get even the least bit of enjoyment from it I had to watch in the nude, which precipitated getting me thrown out of a number of hotel bars. I undressed and watched the segment.

I tried to think where my death would be reported if I were a Larry David murder story.

Bingo.

I had inadvertently switched the channel to an in-room bingo station winning a free drink at the hotel's bar, the Hotel Bar & Orifice, known to the local riffraff as HBO.

Wait a minute. HBO. Of course. If there were any place that would notice Larry's disappearance, it would be HBO. Not only had it become Larry's post-*Seinfeld* home, but he and the former CEO of HBO, Chris Albrecht, had formed such a strong bond that many in the industry felt there was something more than just a business relationship between the two former members of the New York Improvisation comedy club clan. This is not a wink-wink thing. I'm just sayin'.*[23]

Chris Albrecht's position in television had long been seen as untouchable: the head of a network that continued to stand alone at the

---

23 *"I'm just sayin'": *Phrase used with the permission of Paul Reiser and Paul Reiser Enterprises, Ford LTD.*

top, producing far more quality, and what some might call, risk-taking programming, than any other network. Many said Albrecht had the biggest set of balls in the business. Detractors, albeit jealous ones, point to HBO's narrower demographic and pay cable's wider parameters which allowed for, let's say, more adventurous programming. As my grandmother once confided to me on her deathbed, "They show tits, ass and say 'fuck.'" Always a winner. To those non-believers who believe that this is all you need to be successful, I say one word: Starz.

So why is it that little-bitty HBO, with comparatively tiny budgets and seemingly the second or third choice for film and television production companies, scoops up the Emmys and keeps attracting the A-list stars year after year?

I remember meeting Chris at a Palm Springs Pottery Barn and Bordello where he was kind enough to pass on some of his wisdom ... as well as loaning me some sorely-needed baby oil that I had forgotten to pack.

We sat in the steam room, he on a higher bench than I. I must admit that as I listened to his words I was somewhat distracted by – protruding from under his towel – a huge set of balls. That was it. It wasn't just figurative. He actually had a huge set of balls. The most enormous set of balls I had ever seen. Still, when Einstein is about to pass on the secret behind relativity, you don't let humongous testicles get in the way.

"My experience in broadcast television is that you pretty much have to guess what an audience is going to like so that you might be able to put your arms around the largest audience possible," Chris mused. "And in that process, the point of view gets watered down. All our success has stemmed from creators who are also writers and producers who decided to come here and do what is arguably their best work, unique work that they felt couldn't be done anywhere else. They brought with them a point of view, a passion, an intelligence and ability. And they brought with them a commitment to see it through, although the financial pot of gold is arguably at the end of the network and syndication rainbow."

Besides *Curb Your Enthusiasm*, HBO had been the home for historic shows like *Dream On, The Larry Sanders Show, Six Feet Under, The Sopranos* and a whole bunch of others that would have never seen the light of day on the networks. And, I'm just guessing here, but I would be surprised if they don't break records in the future with some sort of *throne gamey* series.

"We look for the opportunity to be more truthful and honest. Now I don't know that other people can't do that, but we choose to, and I think that helps define who we are. The slippery slope of success comes from trying to recreate it. When you start to think there's a formula for that or if something doesn't meet up to expectations, you get cautious and then I think you run the risk of trapping yourself in a very claustrophobic environment. I think taking risks breaks you out of that. Ultimately, the shows that we develop may seem to be a risk, but we feel that we're investing in those creators who have a strong point of view, ones that would be interesting to us. It's really very simple. Hire talented people and help them do their best work. The discussions we have with these talents are not intrusive or inflammatory. We're speaking a common language in the ability to refer back to something they said in the original meeting that sparked us."

"Should I pour more water on the hot rocks?" I asked, hoping that Chris would think me bold and unique.

"Sure," he said. "Go ahead."

I wanted Chris to remember this courageous moment so that I might use it as a springboard to a creative pitch at a more appropriate and decently-clothed occasion.

I filled up a pitcher of water from the hose and poured it on the rocks, filling the room with newly minted steam.

"Why don't you choose to do what network executives do and use your expertise to tell the showrunner what they must do to make the show work?" I asked, looking away, hoping he hadn't noticed that I had tried to catch another glimpse of his enormous, protruding sack. It had nothing to do with sexuality or any sort of sensuality. It was more like the sensation you felt when you walked through Ripley's Believe It or Not and laid eyes on the two-headed calf. It was just, "wow."

"Having worked with top talent a very long time, I'm very tentative about saying things that I think would inspire them. I also know how a lot of different ideas can take what could be a very good show and make it a mediocre show. To me the worst meeting is the one where I have the best ideas."

I almost choked on that one.

"That seems to be the direct opposite of what network execu..."

"I'm not writing the show," Chris interrupted. "I'm not acting in the show. I'm not producing the show. I'm not in the editing room. I'm not doing the sound mixing."

"Don't you do anything?"

"So it doesn't matter if my idea is a good idea or not," he said quite rightly ignoring my snark. "What we have to do is not change or intrude on the process as much as we sometimes have to aid them in ways like reminding them that 'this isn't what we originally talked about,' or 'I don't like this casting,' because by this time we've established a criteria for making decisions that everyone agreed on, one that the creative person can rely on, one which was actually their idea. What you're actually doing is saying 'I want to do what you said you wanted to do.'"

And then he abruptly stood up, *dropped the mic* and walked out. The man had passed on his genius, took himself along with his gargantuan gonads and exited stage left (or right) – I never know whether you base the stage side on the audience's POV or the actors'. It's a bit like the confusion I have with baseball trying to figure from whose perspective are right, center and left field designated. Center is toughest to figure as the player surveying centerfield is the one most likely to take fly balls hit to left center or right center. Very selfish. There needs to be some kind of rule book to explain this. But obviously they could care less.

But wow.

If anyone would be aware of Larry David's unfortunate demise, it would be Chris.

I was about to place a call to his Century City offices when there was a knock at the door. Who could that be? No one knew I was here except the desk clerk and, I guess, the slight, young Latina maid who was kind enough to, how you Americans say, *puff up my pillow* – twice, the night before.

I peeked through the drapes and there stood the maid, with three young children and behind them, an older Latino man and woman who looked just like the maid, but older and weightier, though still fetching. The man was holding a large trunk. Omigawd. The connubial gift. They were there to have me marry their daughter.

Christ! I'm already married, albeit to a former maid from a motel I stayed in long ago. I can't marry another maid. My sheets are already too taut and I couldn't fit another towel animal in my bedroom.

Damn. *Better part of valor*, I said to myself. *Better part of valor. Do the right thing, Steve. Do the right thing.*

Then almost immediately thereafter, *I have got to get the fuck out of here* and *I'm climbing out the fucking bathroom window,* severely drowning out any remnant of *Do the right thing.*

I attempted to escape out the window and a few moments later I soon found myself bleeding profusely as I had forgotten that I was exiting from a second-floor room. Limping severely, I circled the motel hoping to get into my car in the front parking lot without anyone seeing me. 'Course, it would have helped if I had actually driven there. My car was still at Larry's place or in police custody, whichever came first.

In any event, sitting in a car in the motel parking lot were two large gentlemen wearing identical Brooks Brothers suits which were obviously greatly influenced by the *Men in Black* film series, though their sunglasses were more faux-diamond encrusted in a light-purple plastic *Pricilla,*

Queen of the Desert setting than they were *Men-In-Blackish.* They shared one pair of binoculars as they eyed the future Latino mishpuchah at my motel room door.

I didn't think they were there to back up the maid's right to my soul. Shit. It didn't matter that the media had seemingly ignored Larry's murder. I was being hunted by people who didn't really know who I was as well as whom I knew not. Convoluted, but at this point, everything was.

What to do? What to do?

That's when I heard the light and lilting tones of Rod Serling.

I was receiving a text.

From "LD."

Larry David?

Reaching out from beyond?

Whoa!

CHAPTER TWELVE

What Does GO 27000 Mean?

The text read…

Go 27000 West Third ... Lower Lot. L.D.

Go 27000 West Third ... Lower Lot? What did that mean? Could it really have been from Larry? Dead Larry. I pressed *69 but found that I hadn't bought that redial option when I chose the *For Those on A Budget* plan. Damn you, Verizon! Damn you, my inbred cost efficiency.

Go 27000 West Third ... Lower Lot. I had taken a minor in cryptology in college. I flunked it, but the entire process of numerology, paradigms and mixed-up-meaningology always held a fascination for me.

From the crude markings on the cave walls to the crude markings on public bathroom walls, what some may see as just mindless graffiti, cryptology has been an oft-used method to conceal information from undesirable minds and eyes not privy to the keys needed to interpret the seemingly senseless scribblings.

Pig-Latin, the pulling of the first letter of a word, sticking the suffix "ay" or "ae" on it then ferrying it to the end of the word, has long been a cryptic technique used by many elementary school children. For example, the word "anatomical" in pig-Latin would become "natomicalay," though probably a bad example. In any event, it is only when elementary school children speak to their parents where short-term memory loss makes pig-Latin a viable option for kids to hide the fact that they're fucking with your head.

Of course during war time the cryptic messages from the government and military intelligence were much more intricate. For example, in 1968, during the Viet Nam war era, Presidential candidate Richard Nixon said, "I know how to end the war and if you elect me I will reveal my plan." The American electorate who voted Nixon into office was obviously unable to decipher the hidden message in his words until after he was elected. They were, "I have no idea and if I did, I'm certainly not going to reveal it until I beat the shit out of that pantywaist, WWII hero, McGovern." Can't confirm this but I think he added, "I like my military heroes who were not caught being heroes."

The manner of interpreting any of these messages involves breaking it down to its barest root pattern, then taking every historical and themed reference that might apply, devoting hours, days, and many times, years to uncover its actual meaning.

It would look like "Go 27000 West Third ... Lower Level 10 A.M." was just one of those conundrums.

Wait just a minute. What if "Go" meant "Go" and "27000 West Third ... Lower Level" was actually "*to* 7000 West Third ... Lower Level," then the message could have meant, "Go to 7000 West Third ... Lower Level 10 A.M."

Wow. And they say one semester of community college doesn't pay.

7000 West Third is the address of the Writers Guild of America in Los Angeles and I just happen to be a member. That's where my residuals, the ones that were so minimal they jangled in my pocket, were sent from. But, believe me, I am still thrilled that I get to see WGA nominated films for free from November to February. *[24]

---

24 *Just in case any WGA officials are reading this, they should know that in no way would I take get a free ticket to a nominated film and instead see another film. Nor would I use a large popcorn bag that I had from a previous visit to get a free refill.*

Just as the information sunk in, "Go 27000 West Third ... Lower Level 10AM," the next text came through.

"O, Draconian devil!

Oh, lame saint!"

Even the most novice staff writer on a Saturday morning animated show would recognize the meaning. It was a perfect anagram of ...

"To find Larry!

You must find me!"

Okay, it wasn't a perfect anagram. I had to change a few letters to have it make any sense, but still ....

Was it really from Larry David? Unlikely, unless Larry had recovered nicely from his homicidal battering.

I had no idea who sent me the message. It could have been someone who wanted to help. Then again it could have been a set up.

At this point, with no one to turn to (I had long ago lost contact with anyone I had given reason to trust me), I figured I had nothing to lose.

CHAPTER THIRTEEN

The Writers Guild –
Jobs 'Rn't Us

I stared up at the Writers Guild of America building, the Los Angeles home of the union for those writers who have worked for television shows and films whose producers are signatories to the Guild.

A classic example of architectural risqué, the ultra-modern, four-story building had only three floors and – dedicated to the art form it represents – it was built completely out of unintelligible film scripts from novice screenwriters who paid $20 to register their heart-wrenching, years-in-the-writing, soliloquies that had absolutely no chance of ever seeing the light of day, let alone the light of a theater screen.

It could have been worse. The original blueprint called for two exciting and intensely entertaining floors with steps leading to a final, fully satisfying and unpredictable third floor. Unfortunately, notes from a major studio development executive attached to the project suggested that the structure be transformed from a modern office building into a series of unnecessary sexual beats prolonged by a need for speed and a clichéd third floor chase scene that could be turned into an attractive vehicle for Vin Diesel. Luckily, the development executive was promoted to studio head where he was summarily dismissed and his building concept went into turnaround. Without studio input the building went up in record time.

I walked into the building and took the elevator down reaching the lower garage level, the clock reading 9:50. As an unemployed writer I was used to showing up at least ten minutes before scheduled meeting time so that I could get a complimentary Diet Coke early enough to be able to garner a second DC during the actual meeting.*[25]

I stood there feeling naked as the day I arrived in town and had my first real Hollywood pitch meeting with legendary talent manager Harry Miller who told me that the great writers always pitched in the nude.

"Nervous, Steve?"

I turned around, white as a sheet… a white sheet.

"Sorry to creep up on you like that."

Standing there was not Larry, but someone so close to Larry that he could have been Larry's personal neurosis. It was Richard Lewis, comedian extraordinaire, Larry's best friend on *Curb Your Enthusiasm*, star of the Academy Award winning classic, *Robin Hood Can Barely Fit into Those Stretchpants* and Larry's fourth best friend in real life.

Richard had once been Larry's best friend until that one tragic Passover at Albert Brooks' house where Richard distracted Larry from finding the afikomen*[26] by hollering "Haman" as loud as he could just before Larry was about to discover the valuable (sometimes, Brooks was known to give the finder as much as $5) square of matzo. The diversion allowed Lewis's fictional son to score the afikomen reward. Since that time, Bob Einstein (Albert's brother), disgraced major leaguer, Ryan Braun, and SNL writer extraordinaire, Alan Zweibel – all Jews of Note (JON) – moved ahead of Lewis on the David friend scale.

---

25 *In the lesser production companies, the closest to a Diet Coke would be an RC Cola or a Fanta… not even diet.*

26 Aficomen, *a piece of matzo broken off by the leader of a Passover Seder: it is hidden by the leader and later searched for by the children, with the finder, usually the youngest, receiving a reward.*

"Richard Lewis," I gushed like a schoolgirl, you know, in skimpy white panties.

At least I thought it was Lewis. It could have just been a black suit on a hanger. No, wait, it was him.

"You're pretty fucked, aren't you Steve?"

I was delighted that he knew my name.

"You texted me?"

"Yes, I did."

"But my screen said it was from 'L.D.'"

"Yep. Lewis, Dick."

"Dick? You call yourself, 'Dick?'"

"If I want. Would you have come if I wrote R.L.?"

"If I knew it was you? Damn right. I mean, you're the man. Not the only man, of course. But one of them and a pretty significant…"

"Hey asshole," Lewis interrupted. "I'm late for my therapist appointment and today is my bi-weekly colon-cleansing meeting, so let's make this quick."

"David is dead, right?"

"Schmuck. That's what they want us to believe."

They? Us? Lewis was hurling plural pronouns at me right and left, faster than them, we or youse could have thrown.

"Who's 'they?' Who's 'us?'"

"We really shouldn't be doing this here. Too many floors."

What the hell did that mean?

"Let's go across the street to the Farmers Market and get some coffee." Lewis said.

"How about a Diet Coke?"

I knew this wasn't a pitch meeting, but Lewis could afford to pick up the check.

"Okay. Sure. Whatever."

"Then why not."

The Farmer's Market is a conclave of indoor/outdoor greasy food spots where everyone from Oscar winning writers to wannabes named Oscar gathered to discuss how the business was fucking them.

I sat down inconspicuously. I'm a writer. It was the only way I could sit.

"Who is *they*?" I asked.

"Don't you mean 'Who ARE they?'"

Nailed by one of the best.

Lewis was a great comedian, but it is little known that before Lewis took his psychoses to the stage, he was professor emeritus of English at Cambridge's DeVry University.

"I never get it straight. I mean, is it 'who' that affects the verb or is it 'they?'"

"Actually, it's 'what,'" he chuckled. "It's more of a group, an organization."

I was lost and Lewis could tell.

"Drink your Diet Coke (by now I think you can pretty much tell that I've got a pretty hefty product placement deal with Coca-Cola for this book. I'm not ashamed. It's business.). If you shut up for a second I'll try to explain."

"Have you ever heard of the Priory Hegumens Legion of Extreme Mediocrity?"

"Sure. PHLEM. A so-called secret consortium set up to control the quality of world-wide commodities. I think they used it in one of those films *Mystery 3000 Theater* ripped apart. It's a myth, right?"

"Really? You think they're a myth? Are you that thick?"

"Wait. Are you saying that there are powerful people who really control the quality of our products, services and therefore our lives for their own personal profit?"

Lewis gave me one of those incredulous looks that women in singles bars – who I'd think were begging for someone to hit on them – gave me when I approached them. I'd never forget setting eyes on the most beautiful girl I had ever seen and figured if there was ever a time to challenge the fear of rejection this would be it.

"Would you like to dance?" I had asked, confidently, albeit an uncertain confidence.

"Sure," she smiled.

Yes!

"But not with you."

Then again…

From that time on, the word "undesirable" became my lifetime dance partner.

"PHLEM does exist," said Lewis, sharply "although they're just as happy that no one knows. They're hands are dirty."

I couldn't conceal my giggle.

"Don't you mean *their*?" I asked, smugly.

"What?"

"You said, 'they're' which is the contraction for 'they are,'" I said, trying to alleviate any embarrassment he might have felt. "I'm sure you meant to say *their*. It's a common mistake. I wouldn't worry."

He just stared at me like I was some kind of idiot. But really, *they're* instead of *their*. Who was the idiot?

"As I said … THEIR hands were dirty."

"Better," I assured him.

"Dirty as a mom's hand changing a diarrhea diaper in the dark of two in the morning," he said.

And that, ladies and gentlemen, is why Richard Lewis was the man.

"And the proof that they have dirty hands shows up in the place they can reach more Americans than anyone?"

"A Kardashian's vagina?"

I'll admit, it was a hack joke. Too easy and could have used a rim shot. But really, Lewis was the one who threw the softball. I just hit it out of the park, albeit a generic, derivative minor league park.

"Television," Lewis said with impatience seeping from every corner of his exasperation.

"There are powerful people who control television?"

Again with the look.

"It's a hand dealt from the bottom of deck. The Big Lie: A lie that not only affects the welfare of gullible viewers, but also the welfare of every single person working in *the business*. Do you understand how fucked up this is? Do you realize how far these people will go to make sure this doesn't get out? If the public ever got wind of the crapola they're pulling 90% of the network executives would find themselves in the unemployment line where they would be beaten into a bloody pulp by the writers and actors standing in the same line. There would be no more need for 'development' departments because audiences would find out that the shows and scripts written by the original writers were better than the shows after network notes were shoved down the freaked-out, show-running writers' throats."

"But what about the great shows? If what you say is true, how did they make it on to the air?"

"I went to parties where Hugh Hefner would bring in writers – some communists, others very tall – through the rear door. They'd talk about the good times before color TV and multiple orgasms. Things would squeak through, especially in the early days. Everything was so new. Development people had yet to figure out just how to fuck up a show. But when they started to realize that they could get their words and ideas into a script without needing to have an original thought or even writing a word, network executives began to put their bullshit fingerprints on every decent idea a writer tried to get in."

Lewis's anger was beginning to show. I hurried and ordered another Diet Coke just in case he ended our meeting abruptly.

"But when a good show with original stories and concept-breakthroughs broke through to the audiences, those writers who had created them would be hurried off to *cursory* jobs, film or entirely out of the business."

He took a deep, sad breath.

"Carl Reiner, creator of *The Dick Van Dyke Show*, was pushed into valet parking for film premieres at Grauman's Chinese. Norman Lear, the brains and passion behind Archie Bunker and *All in the Family* was considered so dangerous that PHLEM shut him out of the entertainment field entirely. Lear ended up stenciling addresses on suburban curbs as a means to make a living.

"Good writers were snubbed and never heard from again. *That Was The Week That Was*, the early 60's British-based show that created, then immediately broke the mold for, social and political satire, and featured comedy rookies like (in alphabetical order by name) Alan Alda, Steve Allen, Woody Allen, Art Carney, Bill Cosby, David Frost, Buck Henry, Elaine May, Mike Nichols, Louis Nye and Mort Sahl, was written by Robert Emmett."

"Robert Emmett? I never heard of him."

"Eh?" Lewis articulated with raised eyebrows a few inches above a smirk. "Point made?"

"What about *The Daily Show*? That show is funny weekday after weekday ... except for Fridays when Comedy Central runs some generic stand-up comedy piece of shit special. Course, I have no idea how good it would be if Stewart left the show *[27] You could only hope that anyone from South Africa watches the show."

"Sh-h-h. Be quiet. The walls have ears."

"We're sitting outside. There are no walls."

"There are those who don't know that *The Daily Show* is a fake news show."

"How could they know not that ...?"

"The walls ..." Lewis interrupted, once again his soft and subtle finger perched against my lips.

"But I've seen network shows that have had clever spins. What about *Saturday Night Live*? Not now. You know, in the 70s, when it was funny."

"Network sketch shows like *SNL*, *MAD TV*[*28] and the best of them all, *SCTV*, were slotted to play late on weekend nights when viewers were drunk or passed out. The networks just used the shows' acronyms; so, no one really knew what they were."

Lewis was only getting started.

"Now this isn't to say that there aren't hundreds, er, tens of those writers who believe their work isn't hilarious."

It still didn't make sense.

"Really, humor is subjective," I said. "I've watched sitcoms and I've heard the laughter. I'm not speaking about the canned laughter. Someone must find these shows funny."

"Come on, Steve. You know those forced laughs come from staff writers and producers were meant only as cues to the audience to give their

---

27 *He did and then came back, sort of.*

28 *MAD TV is sometimes confused with the magazine MAD or the word "mad" as in being crazy, but FOX (as in "crazy as a… ") drew the acronym M.A.D. from "My Ass-backwards Dandy" a British import that followed the travails of dancer Johnny Slerve, Broadway's only known hetero-sexual hoofer. The rational and meaning of the "TV" part of MAD TV remains a mystery.*

material a chance. In some cases, it works. Hence the phenomena and success of *King of Queens*."

I knew about producers and writers forced laughter pushing their punchlines, but Lewis explaining it was like listening to a great lounge singer, I mean acapella without a decent melody. Basically, I loved listening to him.

"When – and there are certainly *whens* – there was a hint of good writing, those writers were *'splained* that it would better for them if they ceased and desisted. Those who were deemed too difficult or *talented* to control were shipped off to animation or cable where the network bosses expected those writers would die or end up in a fetal position writing questions for the Game Show Network."

"I love the Game Show Network."

"What the assholes never saw coming was the 1980's Animation Revelation where writers discovered how to combine what seemed like two incompatible systems to create a completely new system… one similar to putting pineapple on a pizza: Adult cartoons.

"There were earlier film projects – *Felix the Cat* (X-rated), *Roger Rabbit, Sarah Silverman* – created to push the animation envelope, but these were really just pathetic attempts to make cartoon women masturbatory fantasies for post-pubescent boys or comics on the road who could not afford the Internet or National Geographic. It came from total frustration with the idiotic fixed limits of television half-hour shows. The Animation Revelation allowed writers to massage their inner muse as slowly or rapidly as they desired until, uncontainable and hot, it exploded on the page – sometimes in a partner's hair – uninhibited by Mother Network walking in on the creative process."

"Are we still talking about writing?"

"That's how we got *The Simpsons*, which came from the planting of Matt Groening's gifted seamen deep into Tracey Uhlman's programming uterus; *South Park*, a cartoon that allowed toddlers to curse by not permitting anyone over eighteen to understand the character's apparent mumblings; and *Family Guy*, a program that the networks didn't even realize was animated until the third season."

It was almost too much to digest. *Family Guy* was a cartoon?

"Other sharp comedy writers were shipped off to the Internet, which, in fact, was created, not by Al Gore, but by a television programming vice president who needed an outlet for his stash of hundreds of adorable underage kitty videos. TV executives hoped that top creative talent would stay away from writing clever material for television and instead create content on the Internet where they would be more easily discredited as nare d'wells and nuts. Newsmax and Breitbart themselves were ingenious satirical sites that many thought were real which kept their dark humor from being taken seriously, except by those with a bottomless depth of wit."

"But why?" I asked. "Why would television and the powers in charge want to put out garbage? It makes no sense."

Lewis glanced about checking for network interlopers, then leaned in.

"DaVinci once said 'Many have made a trade of delusions and false miracles, deceiving the ill-advised multitude.' Then again, maybe he didn't say it. He could have just written it."

"And that means ...?"

"Television has made a concerted effort to *dumb down* America."

"Wow. Television isn't interested in benefiting humanity?"

If Lewis rolled his eyes any greater, they would have rolled clean out of their sockets.

"And the powers behind advertising, Big Pharma, fast food, military industrial complex, tobacco, government agencies, the lords of loud of talk radio and many more influential groups have taken full advantage of it."

That I already knew.

"Did you know that it was once said that advertising is the science of arresting human intelligence long enough to get money from it?

"Wait a minute, was that said by economist Stephen Leacock close to a hundred years ago?"

"How do you know that?"

"It's Economy 101. You don't go as far as I have in paying one credit card balance off with another credit card ten times over without some basic economic expertise. Even more extraordinary, very few people know that Leacock was the first economist who used the phrase, 'Do these pants make me look fat?' It led to countless husbands, many not accountants, to give up lucid conversations with their spouses."

Lewis interrupted with a quieting finger to my lips placed in such a manner that I wished he was a twenty-year-old harlot who longed for me to stop speaking so that we might make love. But Lewis had a much different, less erogenous message, a message that threw me for such a disconcerting number of loops that if I had been a thin roll of soft, salted dough, I could have been mistaken for a pretzel. Not a hard, narrow pretzel, but a Philly-based, soft pretzel in dire need of mustard… yellow. Wait, no… brown. Yes, brown it is.

"Power eliminates the need for reason."

"No," I said in disbelief, drenched liberally with a palpable French accent.

Lewis nodded, slowly, intently, removing all possibility that I had misunderstood.

"You're saying that there are people so powerful they don't think they need to explain their actions, no matter how asinine, no matter how unscrupulous, no matter how horrid the means to an end?"

Lewis nodded.

"We're talking government here, right?

"I wasn't, but you're on the right track. The thing is, government doesn't actually run the government. It's a front for those really in power."

"Un-fucking-believable," I said without the "fucking" part, though believe me, I wanted to say it. "But what does all this have to do with Larry David's murder?"

Lewis took a deep breath, straining his neck, checking again for eavesdroppers. His eyes darkened as if Ghirardelli dark chocolate had entered his body.

"Do you remember the missing minutes from the Nixon tapes?"

CHAPTER FOURTEEN

Meanwhile, Back in the Jungle

Ztivo, his blood-soaked thighs exposed, sat naked on a hard wooden chair in the middle of a large, abandoned warehouse, the chair and the room far different from the cushy confines he once ruled as the most powerful of the powerful.

The air was cold. Cold as Ztivo was when he was the coldest of the cold stalking the floors of CAA, freezing out friends and icing his enemies. So cold that Ztivo found his manhood seeking shelter deep within his groin, replicating one character's involuntary penis concealment in the classic "Shrinkage" episode of a not very well-known series.

In a large circle surrounding Ztivo, stood a group of hooded, black-cloaked figures, similar to the figures who stood around and about Tom Cruise in Stanley Kubrick's final film, "Eyes Wide Shut," a film so frighteningly long that it is still not over.

High above the eerie ceremony, hung a large metal plaque of two knights riding upon a single horse. The inscription, "Sigilum Militum Xpisti," which translates as "Seal of the Army of Christ," surrounded the men. The traditional seal of the Knights Templar, it expressed homage to the vows of poverty taken by the order in its early days.

The Knights Templar was a monastic military order formed at the end of the First Crusade with the mandate of protecting Christian pilgrims on route to the Holy Land. The Templars fought alongside King Richard I (Richard the Lion Hearted ... back in the days before they transplanted human hearts) and other Crusaders in the battles for the Holy Lands.

Pursued for their great wealth and moneylending efforts, the Templars essentially invented the banking system, with the establishment of the first ever Citibank, which was soon after renamed Wells Fargo when arena and temple corporate sponsorship became the rage.

Politically, they were influential, immune from any authority other than the Pope. Their bizarre rituals eventually led to their undoing with The King of France, threatened by the Knights' seeming omnipotence, having them arrested for disloyalty whereupon he appropriated their holdings. And with it, foreclosure was born.

You would have thought that the hooded assemblage below was some extension of the Knights Templar if not for the words inscribed directly next to the Templar symbol.

"The Knights Templar or anyone affiliated with said Templar group in whole or part, have nothing to do with those who meet here."®

Identities of those swaying to the slow strands of some indistinguishable, baroque melody or perhaps a Sarah McGoughlin dirge*[29] were concealed by facial masks. To those unversed in the ways of the occult, these macabre facades might have appeared as only incredibly poor examples of cosmetic surgery sought through ads in the L.A. Weekly rather than the astute referrals one can easily attain at a decent Hadassah meeting. But an educated eye could not miss the rubber bands holding the soft plastic, facial veneers in place. These were not results of some extreme makeover. These were incredible masks.

There was no mistaking the identities of the faces painted on each masque. Sid Caesar, Jackie Gleason, Ernie Kovacs, Phil Silvers, Dick

---

29 *I have got to remember to make this month's donation. That dog's sorrowful eyes had burned a hole in my heart. I thought it was a clogged artery. My cardiologist said it was actually 4th stage "empathy."*

Van Dyke, Joan Davis, George Burns, Gracie Allen, Steve Allen, Jack Benny, Oscar Levant, Soupy Sales, Amos & Andy (the black ones), Strom Thurmond and so many more great comedic performers from early television; all of whom benefited from the genius of great comedy writers, all of whose names escape me right now.

The music continued to flow solemnly from the walls, barren except for burning torches strewn systemically. A muddled chant emanating from the hooded figures made the melody all the more ominous.

"Si-i-i-i-i-it...

Ri-i-i-i-ight...

Ba-a-a-a-ck...

A-n-n-n-n-nd...

We-e-e-e'll...

Te-e-e-e-ell...

A-a-a-a-a-a...

Ta-a-a-a-ale...

A-a-a-a-a-a...

Ta-a-a-a-ale...

O-o-o-o-of...

A-a-a-a-a-a...

Fa-a-a-a-te...

Fu-u-u-u-ul...

Tri-i-i-i-i-ip..."

Holey moley. It was the theme from *Gilligan's Island*, one of the dumbest shows of all time. Despite its simple-minded, one note concept, *GI* received great ratings. To this day, people speak fondly of show, Gilligan, aka Maynard Krebs, and the Skipper too ♪

I still think it was more Tina Louise who endeared the 14–99-year-old, heterosexual, male demo that blew away the competition… and sadly, with it, the adorable, school teacheresque Dawn Wells.

As the wearisome, yet catchy chant droned on, the one who seemed to be the leader stepped up to Ztivo and held out his ring finger to kiss. As Ztivo leaned over, his lips pursed in full smooch mode, the leader pulled back his hand, snickering.

He stepped back into the circle and then, one by one, each of the other hooded characters stepped up to Ztivo, held out their ring fingers sans rings, for him to kiss. And as their leader did, each in turn would pull their hand back, accompanied by a discernible chuckle. Only when the last to approach him was about to pull away did Ztivo make an effort to grab on, pulling on the fast-departing finger which, of course, caused that person to fart.

"You have done well, Michael," said the leader.

"Thank you, Master."

"Have you the script?"

"Not as yet, Master."

The Master hauled off and whacked Ztivo across the head with such force that one wondered how his head had remained attached to his neck and shoulders.

"Why not?!" demanded the Master.

Ztivo, wiped a trickle of blood forming at the corner of his mouth.

"There are those who conspire to keep it from us."

Whack!

Ztivo's head rocked back from a second blow.

"No excuses!" growled the Master. "I want that script! It cannot … it will not fall into the wrong hands or our many years of struggles will die with us, or should I say, with you."

The Master then slugged Ztivo once again, this time more violently than the first.

Another of the hooded figures pulled back his Strom Thurmond mask to whisper into the Master's ear.

No one could mistake that head nor the reflective properties of his hairless palate.

Barry Diller.

Okay, those of you not in the Hollywood biz may not be familiar with Diller, but believe me he was one of the most formidable programmers and network wheeler dealers of his time.

Competing with the "big three" networks – NBC, ABC and CBS – Diller developed low-cost, so-called *reality* shows like *Cops* and *America's Most Wanted.*[30]

Diller was also behind the so-called alternative and youth-oriented programming such as *In Living Color* (sketch show) and *The Simpsons* (animated) along with the sophisticated and psychologically-complex, issue-oriented *Married ...With Children*, the forerunner to *The View... With Children*.

And, as if the last page and a half of information was unnecessary fill, Diller removed what was actually a second Barry Diller mask revealing the actual culprit... Bill Gates. Not a mask. This was the Microsoft king for real.

Which is when, for absolutely no fathomable reason, Gates' boots fell off, causing his feet to freeze and crash. His feet were quickly rebooted.

---

30 *Years after its inception, "Cops" was revealed to be fully scripted and choreographed by Las Vegas magic man, David Copperfield. "America's Most Wanted" host John Walsh was the original Abu, the Kwik E Mart owner in Matt Groening's "Simpsons." Primarily an animated East Indian character, Walsh's decision to "go human" forced Groening to recast the part of Abu with an actual cartoon figure and the voice of Helen Hunt's ex-husband, Hank Azaria, who was by then dating Marge Simpson.*

"He's had enough," implored Gates, hoping the Master would cease his vicious physical handling of Ztivo.

"He deserves more," sneered the Master.

"Oh," said Gates, who then approached Ztivo and whacked him over the head with a tattered copy of Variety. Not the standard Daily Variety. This was one of those voluminous advertising homages to a particular theme that the paper used to garner advertising from anyone who was anyone to buy an ad thanking everyone else.

"Wow, that's gonna leave a mark," hooted the Master, adopting a catch phrase that was imbedded in most every network sitcom script. The original line was crafted years before by the inimitable Broadway ingénue Rita Rudner, who first used it as a punchline to a joke she told so long ago no one alive today can remember what the actual set-up was. Breaking the stand-up rule of not ever placing your career in jeopardy by using untried material, during her fourteen-year run at Las Vegas's New York, New York Hotel, the radiant and quasi-brilliant, Ms. Rudner's ninety minute set was made up of completely new material every night. The only exception was her big JFK memorial comedy show on November 23, 2003 (second show) where Rudner, known to those on the inside as the female Julia Roberts, was requested to do her renowned "Sometimes, they leave skid-marks," routine. Soon after that show she told Larry King that she would never tell the joke again, whereupon King asked her to tell the "skid-marks" joke. True to her word, the grande dame of comedy glam, refused.

"What have you to say for yourself?" the Master asked through a sneer.

A bloodied and battered Ztivo rose to speak. A hush fell over the room. A hush so effective, that nary a sound could be heard, 'cept for when one spoke or shuffled a deck of those free playing cards the airlines used to hand out years before they began charging for baggage.

In a voice, hardly discernible above the hush that had now increased to a loud muffle, Ztivo whispered hoarsely, "They are gone."

CHAPTER FIFTEEN

Another One Bites the Dust

"The missing eighteen minutes from Nixon's Oval Office secretly recorded tapes?" I asked Lewis incredulously. "But that was in the early seventies ..."

Whoa. I had just made one huge AARP rookie mistake. No television writer who'd been in this business for over ten minutes would ever make any reference that might connect him to anything establishing that he might be over thirty years old. What if there had been a network vice president having a lunch with one of the nearby under twenty-five-year-old writers? I had to think fast.

"… which was something my parents talked about all the time."

Whew. That was close.

"But the Nixon tapes incident took place in the early seventies. Wouldn't that mean that Larry David, pre-*Fridays*, was still years from having anyone attractive interested in him?"

"Be patient, my son."

My son? Omigod. Richard Lewis was my dad. I always had a sneaking suspicion that there was a secret my family was keeping from me. It should have been so obvious. Even as a toddler I had a penchant for black onesies. So that's why my so-called *real* father never showed me the type of love I so dearly craved and ....

"It's an expression," interrupted Lewis, who had long been thought to possess psychic powers. "You are not my son."

"Apology accepted."

Always be pro-active.

"I can only tell you that the so-called eighteen minutes missing from the tape were actually twenty-two minutes."

"You're saying that there were four minutes missing from the missing eighteen minutes?"

"No," said Lewis with only the slightest hint of impatience. "I'm saying that there was an additional four minutes missing above and beyond the eighteen minutes that were missing."

"Let's me get this straight. Four minutes of tape are missing from the same missing tape that had the missing eighteen minutes? Isn't that, in a way, a double-negative leading one to conclude those additional four minutes, added to the negative eighteen minutes, would result in only fourteen missing minutes?"

"Listen ..." demanded Lewis.

Okay, now his impatience was palatable.

"The eighteen minutes that were reported missing were not actually eighteen but twenty-two. Leave it at that."

I admit that I had mathematical issues. Perhaps this was the infamous Les Moonvis*[31] power numerical sequence that only those with bank accounts large enough to alleviate fear of repercussion would dare speak: the mathematical series that was the basis of most every programming blunder made at CBS.

Or possibly this derived from the Insufferable Epigraphical Ciphers (IEC) which led to the prodigious arithmetic ciphering (PAC) of Jewish Heavyweight Boxing Champion (JHBC), Max Baer's son, Max Baer Jr., in his tour de force depictions as the ignitable, hulking Jethro on the first ever

---

31 *A phony name created to feebly camouflage CBS kingpin Les Moonves hopefully dodging legal repercussions. Of course that would actually work better if I hadn't explained, but alas, it is too late to correct due to a tight deadline for this manuscript's delivery.*

reality show, *The Beverly Hillbillies*.*[32] Then again it could have been another derivation of Politically Hedonistic Irrelevancy (PHI), which equates to the number 1.618, repeated three times fast. It is PHI which many believe to be God and Mother Nature's (Those two together? What's that all about?) building block for all that had ever existed is based. Therefore, the ratio of PHI is the mathematical foundation of all reason, except for Disney's television division's development notes, for which there was no reason.

Just then, searing screams erupted from the writers' tables around us. I thought for sure someone had pitched a *clip* show*[33] in the first year of a series.

I turned back to Lewis, but he had disappeared as if thin air had fattened itself on his existence, or some other magnificently clumsy metaphor.

"Brooks is dead!" screamed a nearby, distraught playwright.

"Mel Brooks died?!" I cried out.

"No, not Mel," cried another unemployed writer.

Not Albert Brooks, I wondered, even though I was well aware his actual last name was Einstein.

"No, not Albert," chided Norma, another mind-reading dramatist, I had sworn never to think around.

Foster Brooks died again? How horrible for his family to go through that twice.

"You stupid, stupid man," thought Norma loudly.

32 *The Hebraic bloodline from father Max Sr. to son Max Jr. has remained questionable as Max Sr. was still alive when Max Jr. was named, while Jewish tradition holds that no Jewish child may be named after a living person. Max Jr. has held that he was not named after his father but after another Max Jr. who died during the Jew's Exodus from Egypt. Details of that Max Jr. are sketchy at best.*

33 *Contrived by writer/producers when they'd run out of ideas, a clip show uses excerpts of previous shows in the series and loosely connects them in a contrived story that usually begins with one character saying, "I'll never forget when..."*

"James Brooks is dead!" shrieked another who thankfully thought to reveal the deceased by both first and sir name, clearing up any further confusion as to who had passed on.

"Oh no," cried out one local football aficionado. "The legendary Cincinnati Bengal running back who was later found to be unable to read the simplest of documents even though he had been a graduate of Auburn University. How sad. How sad on so many levels."

"No, no," moaned another writer, who seemed more distraught than anyone. "James Brooks is dead, the famed film and television writer and creator of such grand programs as *Mary Tyler Moore, Taxi, Rhoda* and lest not we forget the brilliant film *Broadcast News* and a not so brilliant, *My Mother the Car* episode.

The sobbing writer collapsed in a puddle of his own tears. Obviously, he was an extremely tiny man with massive tears who had been touched deeply by the creative genius of Mr. Brooks.

"I just pitched him a new series idea," groaned the prone, soggy writer. "Brooks said he was pretty sure he might consider developing it but had yet to show it to anyone else. And there was no paper trail," wailed the petty opportunist. "No paper trail at all."

How come my agent didn't notify me that Brooks was taking pitches? Damn.

Still, James Brooks. Dead. That was unexpected. I grabbed the first person who had brought the grave news.

"What happened?"

"Car accident," said the eye-reddened scribe. "He ran his DeLorean off the Pacific Coast Highway and into the Pacific Ocean which coincidentally had been named after the highway. Can you imagine that?"

No, I couldn't. It was known to most everyone in the industry that Brooks never stepped into an automobile. Distressed profoundly by the death of the family's pet Shiatsu, Bitsy, from a severe and deadly run-over

when a child, Brooks swore to friends that if he was going to die of anything short of natural causes, it would not be in a car accident. From that
day on he never ventured within fifty feet of a car, made even more difficult
by the fact that he spent his late teen years as a member of the legendary
driver, A. J. Foyt's pit crew.

As years went by Brooks would be ferried about by an actual ferry,
forcing the prodigiously successful writer/producer to set up most of his
projects near deep-water wharfs.

How could he possibly let himself die by some type of car-con-
nected accident? It seemed incredibly suspicious, yet it was reported on
the Internet and quickly inserted into his Wikipedia page, so it's not like
you could really question it.

Even more suspicious, two of television's most successful and brilliant writers had died within twenty-four hours of one another.

The caterwauling screenwriters continued their sobbing lament over
their lost brother and potential buyer.

"Are you Steve Young?"

Ah, I thought, someone had actually recognized me from my extra-
gig on *Roseanne* years before.

"Mr. Young?"

"Why, yes. Yes, I am."

"Please come with me," said a police officer, holding open her wallet
revealing a badge.

At that moment I felt as though I should have taken a big sip of my
second Diet Coke. If there be a good reason to be ready for a classic Danny
Thomas, *Make Room for Daddy.* spit-take, this was it. My *fan* was a member
of the Beverly Hills Celebrity Task Force (BHCTF), the elite police corps
developed especially to track down crimes against wealthy personalities.
We had needed something like this for so long. It's not that they can't protect themselves as much as they are really very busy with more important

things. Important things they do so that you and I don't have to do them, whatever they are.

"This won't take long," said the BHCTF officer, who for the first time I realized was a tall, leggy brunette with a body that wouldn't quit. Except for the fact that one ear was inordinately larger than the other, she might have been the most perfect woman I'd ever seen. That is until I saw her partner.

Wowzers! She was even more perfect. Symmetrical ears, both facing forward as if God had wanted to make sure she heard everything.

"What is this about?" I asked.

"It will all be explained downtown," said the even more gorgeous partner with the evenly proportioned ears.

"I didn't kill Brooks," I said, perhaps overreacting and playing my ace card too soon.

"Omigod! Mel Brooks died?!" screamed the uneven ear'd officer.

CHAPTER FIFTEEN

Groaning, I mean, Groening

Ztivo, still bloody, bruised and wearing a large diaper-like diaper, slithered through the underbrush just inside the ten-foot-high ivy-covered walls surrounding a rainbow-coated mansion. Enormous hedges sculpted into the shapes of the celebrated Springfield, USA-based family, the Simpsons, guarded the mansion. Here would live Homer, Marge, Lisa, Bart and Maggie, if they were real people. But they weren't, so instead, their creator, their God or G-d or even god, Matt Groening, spent his days and most of his nights.

With the Simpsons franchise on hiatus, Homer and the kids, who I reiterate, are not real, were off to Haiti for holiday and the perpetual coup d'état. Groening rarely ventured outside his house lest he be eaten by Bobby, the imaginary eight-foot duckbill platypus he had drawn on his doorstep during the first year of the Simpsons. With Bobby ever-patient, waiting voraciously to ambush, Matt remained a prisoner, busily doing what he did every hiatus: drawing himself into an animated vacation.

This was to be the year that Matt took that fictional trip to France that he had promised himself just after the agonizing season that featured Maude Flanders' death. The tragic death of Ned's wife had come as a complete surprise to Ned and Groening, who for some reason had given the reigns of that particular episode to an inebriated Barney Gumble who, during his 45th, no sorry, 46th futile stay at the Betty Ford Clinic, scripted

Maude's devastating fall from the racetrack stands in "Alone Again, Natura-Diddly."

As Groening was amid completing his sabbatical storyboard, outside his house Ztivo lurked, a threat far more deadly than any platypus, no matter how toweringly drawn. With Bobby, now lying lifeless on the porch, next to the doornail that he was as dead as, Groening knew little that this would be the last vacation he didn't actually go on.

CHAPTER SIXTEEN

Beverly Hills Celebrity Task Force

The BHCTF station and cigar lounge is the busiest police bureau in the state. It houses a special police force so large that it has its own special police force, or so I would expect that Henny Youngman would say if not for his timely death.

The sum of celebrity-connected crimes so far outnumbers all other crimes put together (if putting them together was structurally possible), both felonious and misdemeanorious. Charlie Sheen himself has his own wing… the Winning Annex.

I was brought into the investigation room, where once again I was swathed in warmed facial hand towels, then severely latte'd. That's when I was shocked, AGAIN, to find that the head detective who would put me through a blistering interrogation was politically independent talk show host and best-selling author, Bill O'Reilly. Yes, that Bill O'Reilly. That guy is everywhere.*[34]

"Which of my books did you like best?" asked the 6'4" Irish behemoth, impishly.

"All of them," I said, hoping that he wouldn't ask about specific passages as I had read only one page of each book, just so I could honestly

---

34 *Having always thought of himself as America's most powerful protectors and believing Hollywood's elite were at the core of America's demise, O'Reilly's side job was as Beverly Hill's top cop.*

quote something to conservative, um… independent women I had hoped to impress.

"Hmmm," he hummed as it seemed I had put one over on him.

"What say you, Mr. Young, about page twenty-two of *Who's Looking Out For You?*" He grinned like the cat that caught the canary, spitting out tiny bits of yellow feathers as he spoke.

"You mean the *Ten Commandments of Raising Children?*" I said, letting out a clear breath of relief as, odds against odds, he had asked about the one page I had read.

"Yes," he said, resigned that I had probably told the truth. "That's the one."

"In fact, I found it so inspiring that I immediately scraped my own style of parenting to replace it with one written by a self-styled megalomaniac," I said, only later realizing that perhaps I had said too much. Still, I said more.

"Y'know, I think you really got a bad rap with that sexual harassment settlement with your producer and a worse rap when your kids didn't want to live with you after you, allegedly, physically abused your wife."

"I'm sorry," O'Reilly said, obviously distracted. "I was thinking about something brilliantly perceptive I opined on during yesterday's show. What did you just say?"

Whew. I had ducked a big one.

"I said, I found it so inspiring that I immediately scraped my own style of parenting to replace it with one written by a self-styled megalomaniac."

D'oh.

"Splendid, Mr. Young," he said, taking my comment as a compliment. "As you know there have been a curious series of deaths concerning well-known television writers."

"Oh my God. Really? Who?" I asked, feinting disbelief.

THE LARRY DAVID CODE

O'Reilly smiled a shit-eaten grin that his own breath could not disguise.

"James Brooks."

"I heard."

"David Kelley, too."

Oh God. David E. Kelley, creator of the hysterical and legally inept *Ally McBeal, The Practice*, and the incomprehensible *Doogie Howser, M.D.,* was killed?

"How did he die?"

"I was going to ask you the same thing, Mr. Young."

Did O'Reilly think I really knew, or worse, did he somehow think that I had something to do with Kelley's murder?

The leggy officer with the uneven ears came in and leaned over about to whisper to O'Reilly. O'Reilly quickly turned towards the officer, catching her on the lips with a kiss. The officer used her arm to wipe O'Reilly's dripping, mucus-filled saliva from her face and dropped a slip of paper on his lap. Mumbling incoherently, she walked out. O'Reilly peeked at the paper, his grin fading into a dour wince, almost as if he just heard that the latest polls had Al Franken surging ahead in a Republican presidential primary. Letting the paper slip slowly from his fingers, and without as much as a "you have the last word," hand cupped to forehead, he walked from the room.

I picked up the paper and read four agonizing words: Matt Groening's dead.

Three words.

Granted, one was a contraction.

I'm pretty sure Richard Lewis would agree.

CHAPTER SEVENTEEN

Groening Goes on Eternal Hiatus

I sat there, my head spinning like a dreidel being twirled by a drunken eight-year-old who didn't know enough to stop at one glass of Manischewitz concord grape juice. Brooks, Groening, Kelley, aleph, beis, veis, gimmel, not to mention Larry David, who in fact, O'Reilly didn't. What the hell was going on? Brilliant writers were falling faster than another drunken eight-year-old (who had been drinking with the first kid*[35]) tripping over an oversized menorah. Nothing made sense except for the fact that the concurrence of these deaths made no sense at all. I could see them all dying at once if they were all heading to New York for the annual New Fall Season Programming Announcements to the affiliates, flying in the same airplane going from the west coast to the east at 650 mph just as an MTV private jet carrying 300 members of Lil Wayne's posse going 750 mph from east coast to west for the semi-annual Beverly Hills-adjacent booty-call, both leaving at the same time. But there was no evidence of Lil Wayne's collusion in the crimes.

Not yet.

---

35 *Television has proven that no child under the age of thirteen would touch a drink. And I'm not speaking of a Bar Mitzvah sip of wine. I'm talking about downing beer as the thirteen-year-old lead character did in my award-winning script for the "The Smart Guy," a show that confirmed that placing "smart" in the title did not equate to a show's character being smart.*

Nothing I had heard from Richard Lewis seemed to jell with the ghastly events.

David Kelley's death was being ruled a suicide, yet with his inestimable cache' still able to open any door and the fact that he was able to see his wife, Michelle Pfeiffer, naked almost any time he wanted, why would he even consider suicide? Unless … Nah, she couldn't look that much different than she did in clothes. No way this was a suicide any more than Larry David's death was. And still, there wasn't any word of David's death. I saw the body. Someone or something must have connected me to the events.

Yet, Lewis had dropped "That's what they want us to believe," concerning the validity of David's death. What could that possibly mean?

I could see out the two-way mirror where several officers were huddled with O'Reilly and pointing in my direction. The mirror was supposed to be one of those clever devices that allow the police to look through the interrogation window at perps*[36] being beaten into admissions of guilt, while the perp himself would only see himself in the mirror. But at the BHCTF, the two-way mirror was just a regular window. This was a standard part of the inhumane pressure they would place on their celebrity captives so as to not let them look into anything that might reveal their reflection or image, keeping them incessantly guessing as to how good they looked. In some cases, just to get to a mirror, the celebrity would break down and admit to the crime without even being questioned.

The officers kept looking in my direction and making "slitting throat" and "hanging" gestures then followed it with hysterical laughter.

Shit. This was nuts. I had nothing to do with any of the murders. Why in the world would anyone think so?

Just then my editor, Bobby Slayton, showed up. I was saved. Slayton would vouch for what a pussy I was and how my lack of any decent

36 *Short for "perpetrator" which could have easily been used so there would be no necessity for a footnote, but how many times in a comedy writer's life does he get to use the word "perp?"

relationships in the industry kept me from ever getting close enough to any of the recently-departed, literary stars.

O'Reilly nodded and seemed to be sold on whatever alibi Slayton was giving him to explain my innocence.

O'Reilly came back in, I assumed, to say I could go.

He clutched a legal note pad. A legal one. Not one of those black market, litigious-risky note pads made from infectious maple leaves smuggled in from Canada.

"Mr. Young," O'Reilly read from his American-made note pad. "Did you ever say, 'If Matt Groening, James Brooks and a few hundred writers under the age of thirty committed suicide, maybe then some show would hire you'?"

Omigod. I had said that. It had been a joke. Not a good one, mind you. Need proof it wasn't any good? I sold it to Leno as part of his "Tonight Show" monologue.

"It was a joke." My voice shivered like a dog that had just been pulled from a frozen lake.

"Not very funny, Mr. Young," O'Reilly scowled as he wiped off the lake water I had shaken off.

"It was more ironic, not funny," I explained. "Irony doesn't necessarily evoke laughter."

I was grasping at straws.

Last straws.

"It was meant to express the opposite," I pleaded. "Haven't you ever read Jonathan Swift?"

"I went to Yale, Mr. Young. I've read everything."

"Then surely, you're smart enough to know what irony is. Like when you say people are 'really smart' but you mean they're just plain dense."

"So, you think I'm dense."

"Bad example," I admitted.

"Very funny, Mr. Young. Or should I say 'ironic.'"

"You could. But that's my point. Sometimes it's difficult to tell the difference between the truth and a joke."

"If suddenly, all the writers in Hollywood died, except for you, you'd pretty much be in the driver's seat, wouldn't you, Mr. Young?"

He had me there, though if that were true and with the bucks, I'd then be pulling in I don't think I'd ever have to be in the driver's seat. At least not in the limo with my driver, Bitteman, handling the wheel. Still, I was starting to believe that I had killed these guys. And if I hadn't, I was starting to think that I should have… a long time ago.

"Or am I just being ironic, Mr. Young? Go ahead, you have the last word."

I sat there, unable to speak. Still, they would need more than just a weak joke expressed privately to hold me.

"I was really a fan of Art Carney…."

"What?" asked O'Reilly.

"And Jerry Lewis."

"What the hell are you talking about?"

It was just a shot in the dark, but I figured if I threw out enough names I would throw O'Reilly off.

"And you can't forget about Lou Costello. You know, Abbott and Costello. Abbott was the tall, skinny one. All pretty funny guys. Wish I could have written for them."

"You're nuts."

It was working. Perhaps I would get off with an insanity plea.

"Lock 'im up, boys," demanded O'Reilly.

Maybe not.

CHAPTER EIGHTEEN

Clank

Do you realize how much you can do with a 12X12 cell? I don't. At best, mine was 6X6. Just a bit larger than a walk-in closet. And it was dark. Dark as a starless night at Spago.

"Young. Out of the closet," demanded the large, burly, but extremely friendly guard.

It seems the BHCTF cells, or "cell suites," were each equipped with walk-in closets and living space fashionably designed with the modern celebrity prisoner in mind. Besides the king-sized cot and Blue Tooth DVR, each inmate was assigned a personal secretary for responding to autograph or peer-prisoner cigarette requests, setting up prison lunch meetings and exercise yard photo-ops. When they realized that I was only a writer, Brock, my beloved production assistant, was quickly transferred to the former ICM agent in the next suite who was serving a five-to-ten sentence for returning over-forty-year-old clients' phone calls.

"It's time for your body search," summoned the guard.

I had requested four that day and with the stress I had been put through, this one came none too soon.

As the body search went into its second hour, I began to discover new feelings that I had never known existed before. It became evident that even with this momentary escape from reality, unless I escaped, I might be facing myriad charges for murders I had not committed.

As the guard, who was fast becoming someone I would be adding to my "when I win the Oscar" after-party guest list, was packing his massage table ready to leave the cell, while he wasn't looking, I deftly squeezed into his massage oil portmanteau. Small and a bit more boxy than my first Greenwich Village living quarters, I would bear the discomfort for I would soon to be free as a bird, albeit, a land-bound bird who would shortly be able to run panic-stricken from the coppers.*[37]

During my time in the guard's valise, I thought of what Lewis had said to me. Was there a secret consortium set up to control the quality of world-wide commodities? Was he trying to tell me that PHLEM was behind these literary homicides?

"PHLEM does exist," Lewis had said. "If the public ever got wind of the deceit, 90% of the networks' executive workforce would find themselves in the unemployment line. There would be no more need for *development* departments."

If I was going to find out who was behind these murders, I was going to have to find PHLEM. I would need to figure out why the powers in charge would want to put out bad TV and *dumb down* America.

Then I remembered what DaVinci once wrote...

Many have made a trade of delusions and false miracles,

Deceiving the unwise multitude.

I have seen enough campaign commercials, political speeches and debates to know that without delusions and deceiving we'd lose 90% of the candidates. But there was one question that resonated most.

"Do you remember the missing minutes from the Nixon tapes?"

I had to find out what that was all about.

"Driver. Take me to the Richard Nixon Library and make it snappy," I would have said if I had a driver or was not still stuck in the guard's case.

---

37 *As the apparent target of a massive police search it seemed an apropos time to adopt a modicum of criminal slang, if for nothing else, literary effect.*

I broke open a bottle of rich, massage oil and poured it over every inch of my body, allowing me to slide through the air-hole in the case. Once outside I found myself face to face with a well-known character actor (don't remember his name but you'd recognize him; been in a million things) who luck upon luck was a certified Uber driver who drove to supplement his acting down time. He drove a lot.

He was about to drive me to the Nixon Library, which would save me a ton of money over a standard taxi, when a call came through to the driver. It was for a part in a Woody Allen film. While Allen's films were no longer funny, the lack of humor was augmented by the powerful sense of tedium. Still, you don't turn down Woody.

The driver needed to get to the airport fast triggering one of those story absurdities that you could drive a tandem-axle 80,000 lb. GW tractor through – the kind that you exasperatedly whisper to your wife, "that would never happen," ruining every film she's ever seen with you… um… me. Despite the seeming lack of logic – I swear that it happened – the driver asked me to drive him to the airport in his car. He said I could keep the car but wanted me to promise that I would pick him up when he returned. Being that I was in the middle of a confusing and rather terrifying situation I couldn't commit to picking him up. We settled on my signing an agreement, not so much an agreement as much as a back of a gas receipt, which while I wouldn't guarantee that I'd pick him but would give it a shot if circumstances changed.

CHAPTER NINETEEN

The Nixon Library

I had never been to Orange County, California. It was said to be fraught with rabid conservative, Christian-hugging monsters and the home to healthless iceberg lettuce-based salads. But if I was to find out who or what was behind the Plague of Comedy Writer Murders I was going to have to go deep into enemy territory.

The San Diego Freeway was backed up for miles, I was able to make it around the (Route) 405's normally clogged lanes by legally using the car pool lane having picked up a hitch-hiker who had more than a fleeting resemblance to a bulked up Charleze Theron. After paying the prerequisite $20 and thanking her for a rather indifferent hand job, as well as not killing me, I arrived on the Presidential Library grounds.

Stipulating that I was neither African American nor Jew, I was ushered into the esteemed and disgraced former president's hallowed hall. Bedecked in a Nixon administration theme, every female attendant looked like Pat Nixon. Every man looked like Bobby Haldeman or Johnny Erlichman. The security guard, who held his lit lighter less than an inch from the palm of his hand, was a dead ringer for Gordon Liddy.*[38]

After getting over the fact that the library had not a children's section nor Dewey Decimal System to be found, I was stunned by the piety

---

38 *Later DNA testing of the pieces of charred skin that sparked from his hand proved that this was Gordon Liddy whose radio show had been canceled due to his last remaining listener losing his official Aryans R Us membership.*

I felt walking past the portraits depicting the great moments in the lives of the former president and First Lady (not Pat, but the very first lady... Eve, looking fabulous, who due to a diet of only fruit, 'cepting apples, had outlived Adam by a number of years). It was as if Mel Gibson had nailed my heart to the cross, then used the gushing flood of fresh heart blood to paint a picture of a Jew having his heart pulled out while being nailed to a cross. Heartwarming.

On display were pictures from the earliest moments of Nixon's '68 presidential campaign, when Dick claimed that if elected he would reveal his secret plan to immediately get us out of Viet Nam, next to one of him promising if reelected in '72 he would disclose his secret plan to unequivocally get us out of Viet Nam, next to photos of the National Guard being welcomed onto the Kent State campus represented by hundreds of cheering students (running away), which was next to a diorama depicting fifty-thousand flag-draped coffins being brought home from our honorable victory in Indonesia, sitting next to Nick Ut's photograph of the naked Vietnamese child (Kim Phúc) running away from her bomb-strafed village behind a stack of classified documents proving the *unavoidable* collateral damage from the Mylai Massacre which led to a theater where "All the President's Men," played on a loop which opened with a documentary on the precious marriage of Julie and David Eisenhauer where one couldn't help but be moved by the memories that were rushing through my mind like a tall Starbucks double decaf cappuccino enema that had been mistakenly left in a microwave for twenty minutes, all laid out in a 203 word sentence.

But there was one thing that struck me above all else. That one thing was not what was there, but what wasn't: the famous missing segments of the Nixon Whitehouse tapes. Was there ever eighteen minutes of tape missing or was what was missing something that never existed to be missed? Double negatives were flying through my head like no bullets you never saw.

Just then a library attendant who bore a striking resemblance to former Nixon secretary Rosemary Woods tapped me on the shoulder.

"Follow me," she said in a voice more akin to James Woods than Rosemary.

"But what...?"

She tenderly placed a single, rather hairy finger to my lips, pursing hers in a silent shush.

"You'll find out soon enough," she said un-silently.

She led me past a long line of visitors waiting to view the newly uncovered Nixon collection of conservative hip-hop and pornography into a waiting glass elevator that would take us down deep into the clogged bowels and small colon of the library. We walked past the yet to be publicly-displayed statue of the young, naked Hank Kissinger, which, as fate would have it, was standing right next to a statue of an elderly, naked Kissinger. I soon realized, after a closer inspection of the genitals, this was no statue.

The Woods-like attendant led me through a labyrinth of darkened corridors and onto an elevator. Inside there were only two buttons: H(ere) and T(here). She pushed T and the elevator shot upward with a jerk (actually two jerks counting me – but I tellya), reaching a g-force I thought would suck my head down into my pants. Of course, had that been the fact this story would not need one more word nor would I have the time to spend writing that word. But alas, it would have to remain a descriptive and potentially lurid pictogram.

After a Six-Flag worthy ride, the doors opened to an empty corridor, empty until we stepped into it.

The attendant beckoned me to follow her a few steps and into a small, simple office. Locking the door, she walked lithely across the room, sliding suggestively into a chair behind a prodigious, mahogany desk, lifting her freshly shaved legs onto the desk revealing the dark steamy, environs of her pantiless Y. I didn't have be Bill Clinton to realize that this was not only a come on, but the come on was being delivered by a woman who was no woman I ever learned about in 7th grade health class. As the Kink's "Lola" played through my head, she yanked off her hair (not a wig, her actual hair) followed by a removal of a mask, revealing that this woman, who was beginning to set off a yearning in my loins that I hadn't felt since 7th grade health class, was no woman at all.

She was…

Larry David.

CHAPTER TWENTY

I Mean, __HE__ Was Larry David

Larry David. Not dead. Not on life support. Alive. Just as alive as most people today… who are living.

"You're not dead."

"Aa-ah. Not so much."

"But I thought … I mean I saw your bloodied body."

"Yeah, it's… it's kind of what I wanted you to believe."

"But Richards saw it too."

"Na-ah. Y'don't know that."

"I saw him run from the house."

"How can you be sure?

"Because… because I saw him? With my eyes."

"Did you ever see David Blaine's illusion where he cuts off his arms and legs with a feather from a dove, then lobotomizes himself?"

"Without his arms?"

"He still had his hands."

"Wait. He cut off his arms. Weren't his hands attached to his detached arms?"

"Ah, see that's part of the illusion."

"So, he reattached his hands to what, his shoulders?"

100

"Now you're talking stupid."

"Okay. I have no idea what you're talking about but whatever it is it sounds repulsive."

"Still, think about it. Do you think Blaine really cut off his limbs?"

"Like I said, I never saw it, but my guess is that it only looked like he cut off his arms and legs."

"Exactly."

"So, you're saying Richards was only an illusion."

"I'm saying, you never know. You could have thought it was Richards."

"If it wasn't Richards, who was it?"

"Well… Ever go to an AA meeting? Alcoholics Anonymous."

"Um. Kind of."

"I went once. Y'know, I'm fine with drinking, but I've heard alcoholic women are supposed to be… interesting. There was a lot of… whining. A lot of 'oh, being an alcoholic is the greatest thing that ever happened to me.' You know, losing my job, losing my family, sitting in an unfurnished one-room cardboard box. Most really made no sense. If I told you exactly what they said you wouldn't understand."

"I don't understand."

"See."

"Wasn't that a bloody body in your bed? Was that just a David Blaine illusion?"

"It's the 21st century. I had a simple android built to replace me whenever I was supposed to show up at some stupid show business affair that I couldn't stand to go to. Anyone who's anyone in Hollywood has a closet full of these things. No one really goes to any show biz event."

"Oh, yeah. Sure."

I was way off the grid when it came to technology but I knew that admitting that I was not familiar with what the kids were playing with today was another of the employment-killer ruses that the industry used to trap aged writers facing youthenasia.*[39]

"Trying to make a point here. Did you know that there's a secret group set up to control the quality of almost everything sold around the world?"

"PHLEM," I announced proudly, pleased that I was paying attention to my own narrative.

Larry rolled his eyes, his impatience overriding any shock in my familiarity with PHLEM.

"Right now, our most important American rights are being stripped away by the same people who we elected to protect us from those who attempt to take away those rights?"

"Dreadful, as well as so very difficult to follow."

"So-o-o… I had no choice but to fake my own death."

"You're saying that you faked your own death to save America."

"Exactly."

"That's pretty pretentious, isn't it?"

"Pretentious? You want to hear pretentious? Listen to this…"

Larry tapped his knee requesting me to sit on his lap. I can't say that he had to ask me twice. I climbed on. Larry spoke calmly.

"For the past few months Washington has been holding a sham of a Senate investigation looking into the administration's efforts to repeal EVERY SINGLE FREEDOM. The only one they're leaving alone is the little-known Amendment I (A), known as the *Bowler Bill*.

"I've never heard of it."

Larry pulled a litigious-like document out of his pocket and handed it to me.

---

39 *Youthenasia: The state by which employees under the age of presumed hipness to the under-thirty generation are deemed creatively and intellectually dead to their particular industry. i.e. forty.*

"Read it yourself."

I read it out loud so that you readers can read it here.

"Congress shall make no law respecting the establishment of silly hats nor prohibit the free exercise of the wearing of said inane caps, or abridging the freedom of the wearing of ridiculous headwear, or of the press to report on the donning of these berets, bowlers or fedoras, or the right of the people to assemble peaceably to discuss the wearing of any hat, no matter the ethnicity of origin – though if said hat is other than white, it would be considered no more than 3/5th of a hat."

Thank God our leaders are protecting the rights that separate us from animals. Except for the now extinct Indiana Gentleman Badger, only humans have chosen to wear a hat.

Larry became more agitated, more animated. Just short of transforming into a full-fledged cartoon. He took out a teleprompter and read from it as if he was one of the Founding Fathers, if teleprompters had been developed in the early 1700's, when in fact the FF's actually used antiquated cue cards.

"Every other freedom the Founding Fathers had established was immediately sacked by these politicians who were supposed to oversee protecting our rights. Thomas Jefferson and the other syphilitic, sex-crazed, slave-owning forefathers thought they had planned for most every attack on our rights, making sure the Constitution had every protection. But one they had overlooked left the Constitution with all the power of an old piece of parchment that had no power."

"Wow. You talk real good."

Larry pulled a small CD player and ear buds from his pocket.

"Pretty shocking, right? Tell me I'm right."

"You're right?"

"Gets worse. This CD contains top-secret congressional testimony that was smuggled out of the hearings in a leftover piece of uranium yellow-cake."

After first wiping off the built-up ear wax from the buds I placed them on. Larry was brilliant, but as with many geniuses, good hygiene was an afterthought. My mother was right. My minor in otolaryngology could one day save my life. Okay, saving my life is a stretch but you can never be too careful when you're dealing with potential ear, nose or throat infections.

What I heard changed everything I ever thought about anything. Clearly, I did not have a very strong belief system.

(EXTREMELY SCATCHY RECORDING THAT LUCK UPON LUCK HAD CLOSED CAPTIONS. YES, ON A CD.)

Senator Reed: Mr. Attorney General. Why is it that we should even consider ridding the people of their well-tested protections and rights?

Mr. Attorney General: (Coughing, under his breath) Blowjob.

Senator Reed: I'm sorry. I didn't get that.

Mr. Attorney General: I said, the President believes that the original laws thought to protect our freedoms, actually impede us from enjoying the very freedoms they were created to protect.

Senator Latte': And how would that be, Mr. General?

Mr. Attorney General: Geez. That's a good one. I think you'd have to ask him.

Senator Latte': (Irritable, raising his voice) And who just might be this "him" you speak of, Mr. General?

Mr. Attorney General: The President.

Senator Latte': (Growing even more impatient) The President of what, Mr. General? If that is your name.

Mr. Attorney General: The President of the United States, Senator.

Senator Latte' (Now speaking as if he had a festering boil crowning on his forehead): What am I, pulling teeth here? Just what is this United States you speak of?

Senator Reed: My good friend, the esteemed Senator from the state of Starbuckania, has a good point. Just what or whom is this United States you speak of?

Mr. Attorney General: The country specified between The United Kingdom and Uruguay on airport lists. I'm speaking alphabetically, of course.

Senator Reed: It seems we're just going in circles here, Mr. Attorney General.

Mr. Attorney General: Exactly. And does that not prove the point that the freedoms, so eloquently affixed to the Constitution by the Founding Fathers, need be eliminated. For the most part it will likewise eliminate those damn activist judges who choose to adjudicate cases based on their own biased interpretation of our law, rather than mine.

Senator Latte': We're all pretty much in sync on that one.

Senator Reed: But if we were to eliminate all the laws of the land, wouldn't we then be a lawless land?

Mr. Attorney General: Lawless? Devoid of any law, Sir? Let us not forget the Bowler Bill. That will keep everyone in line.

Senator Reed: Right. Forgot.

Senator Latte': Makes sense to me.

Senator Reed: What about the Second Amendment? We can't pull that out or there'll be widespread confusion as to what a well-regulated militia is.

Mr. Attorney General: You must think Americans are idiots.

(Appropriate pause)

Mr. Attorney General: Senator Reed?

Senator Reed: I'm thinking. I'm thinking.[40]

Senator Reed: Let's vote.

Senator Latte': All in favor of dropping every amendment in the Constitution, raise your hands. (Beat) Higher.

Senator Reed: Let it be known that all senators have raised their hand except for Senator Woorhero.

Senator Woorhero: I'm trying!

Senator Latte': As it is well known, Senator Woorhero lost both arms while covering up a grenade meant for a Lieutenant G. W. Boosh, a National Guard pilot who at the time was working for a political campaign not in Viet Nam. I would ask that Senator Woorhero be allowed to raise his foot to confirm his vote.

Senator Reed: Senator Woorhero. (BEAT) Thank you. It is unanimous.

Senator Latte': Do you have anything else to say, Mr. General?

Mr. Mr. Attorney General: Yes, you're all under arrest.

Wow. This means that the only thing that stood between discarding all the laws of the land was the President's signature and the court challenges from the American Civil Liberties Union. Damn you, ACLU. Damn all four of your acronym's letters.

"Do you understand how bad this is?" Larry asked.

Believe me. I did not need to hear anything else. America was in trouble. And not the kind that comes from tweeting your crotch lumps to unsuspecting cheerleaders. This was big time.

"Sort of," I assured him.

---

40 *"I'm thinking. I'm thinking." This was not actually in the CD but I wanted to pay homage to a 50's mainstay punchline made famous by the venerable Jack Benny that has endured to and through today's sitcoms.*

"It has to be stopped."

"Why don't you just go on television and tell everyone? Better yet, make an adorable kitten who has become best friends with a three-legged goat video and insert a voiceover explaining what's happening."

"Seriously? I'm a Hollywood insider. Americans don't believe successful show biz personalities no matter how many puppies, kittens or giggling babies we use. Ask Matt Damon.

I had seen that that video. Adorable kitty playing with even more adorable baby larva. Thirteen total views.

"If I spoke out against the government it would just come across as white noise to the public and Clear Channel would stop playing my records."

"What's a record?"

Of course I knew what a record was. But I didn't want anyone else to know I knew.

"CDs," Larry said quickly, wiping sweat from his brow as if he just got away with an age-revealing misstep. "I meant they'd stop playing my CDs."

Even Larry David was aware of ageism.

"You've recorded CDs?

"No. I just own a lot, Mostly Indigo Girls and Dixie Chicks. A few old Go-Gos. Lot of girl groups. I just couldn't stand if they took them off the airwaves."

"But why did you set me up?"

"I needed someone with no skin in the game. Someone who could tell the world what has been taking place."

"Me? I'm a writer. I've got credits. Aren't I kind of a Hollywood insider too?"

Larry stared deeply into my eyes, almost into my soul, for one hell of a long, incredulous beat, his clenched face swelling large and red. Then came the uncontrollable laughter.

"You almost had me there," he said, spitting out the words in between hysterical convulsions. "You, a Hollywood insider? That is rich."

It was useless to argue the point. There was something larger at hand. Something that was bigger than my ego, small as it was.

"But I know what you are capable of. That you've been willing to step up when your country needs you. Because there is one thing that holds us together."

"You mean…"

"Yes," Larry said with a solemn nod. "9-11."

CHAPTER TWENTY-ONE

9-11: Revisited

Obviously, Larry knew what only a few in the comedy biz were privy to when our country was attacked on September 11, 2001 by those cowardly/ brave terrorists (depending on whether or not you are Bill Maher) from Al-Qaeda.

In the wake of the tragic assaults, the federal government and the Defense Department went to Hollywood action writers for help in brainstorming possible terrorist plots against American targets. What wasn't known (right up until this very second), is that they also went to Hollywood comedy writers for help.

Me included.

I remember the morning as if it were September 12, 2001.

When I awoke, about to start applying my deep black Clairol for Men, I found a note taped to the bathroom mirror that said I should go to an address and not tell anyone. I don't normally pay attention to notes I haven't written, but this one was different. It was written on official "Your Government Needs You Now" letterhead.

And it was signed by the President… of the United States.

While driving to the location, the NPR radio station I was listening to was interrupted by a voice that addressed me as "Steve." No one had ever talked directly to me from the radio, except for that one time I got through to Howard Stern, so I felt compelled to listen.

Bababooey.

Only later did I find out that it was Bush spokesman, Ari Fleischer, and that he addressed everyone as "Steve." What he had to say sent shivers up my spine.

"We need you, Steve. Your country needs your twisted perspective and ability to set up witty situations that end with satisfying yet unpredictable resolves."

Unpredictable? Obviously he didn't know I wrote sitcoms. He went on to say that President George W. Bush's seeming mispronunciations and malapropos were only an attempt to "get the comedy thing goin'" and that the administration was running against the clock and didn't know when or how the next terrorist attack might come. They believed there to be a significant number of Taliban comics in training who were appearing regularly on "Evening at the Jihad." Suspicions were that Al Qaeda had already started meeting with those comics to develop zany, though thoroughly evil, suicide attack possibilities.

Ari set the agenda. "We've got to beat those evil doers to the punchline."

The words reverberated like a shot of red, white and blue adrenalin. I thought the only possible thing a patriotic comedy writer could think of at a time like that:

Hey, a job!

I floored the car, then had to immediately slam on the brakes as I found myself on Ventura Boulevard during the morning rush. Even more difficult were the orders that said to wear a blindfold so I didn't know where I was driving to.

Some hours later I arrived at a location in Studio City. There I was given another blindfold (to wear over the first blindfold) by a CIA/FBI/NSA/LSMFT-looking gentleman.

The rush of corned beef and kishka smells filled the room and the fact that I heard Paul Williams talking with Jon Voight while Danny

DeVito ordered from the deli counter, I knew I was in Art's Deli in Studio City. I removed my blindfold and was ushered to the large corner table in the back. The back corner table at Art's Deli.

"This must be important," I thought.

Seated about were comedy film writers, episodic staffs, talk show and sketch guys, even the brilliant team behind the Carrot Top phenomena (for those insidious terrorist prop attack possibilities). There were veteran writers of parodies, romantic comedies, black comedies and satire. So dire was the government's need that even comedy writers over the age of thirty were called in to help.

It was one, fucking, enormous table.

Due to the covert nature of the meeting, I can't disclose any of the names of those who showed up, but suffice it to say, seated in the room was the crème de la crème of the comedy world.

With the unfolding comedy writer serial homicides, today many who were at that table, and still alive, would be in danger of assassination.

With no compensation, other than a complimentary car flag and simple honorarium of $18,760.00 (at the time sufficient for a year of WGA health plan coverage), the lords and ladies behind some of Hollywood's biggest jokes, were ready to be funny for our country as well as the territories of Guam and Puerto Rico.

Only those involved with Rob Schneider movies were kept out.

Egos were left at the door, except for show runners with long term guaranteed deals who could afford to hire a writing assistant to carry their egos in with them.

Following a couple hours of lox, light cream cheese and the onioniest bagels you ever tasted, and after fifteen minutes from a warm-up comic I think I once saw at a taping of *Will and Grace,* a G-man in sunglasses and a simple black suit stood up to speak.

"Gentlemen and ladies. Thank you for giving your time and talent in America's greatest time of need. As of today, this project will be known as 'The Comedy Writers Coming Up with Common Defense Ideas Filled With Wacky Scenarios Alliance.'" The TCWCUWCDIFWWSA representative did not identify himself as he wished to remain anonymous due to his embarrassment over not coming up with a more succinct name that might have provided a slicker with an easier to remember acronym. He then introduced Major Lenny Bobby, Commandant at the Army's Simulation, Training and Borscht Belt Command, based in Lake Titicaca, Florida.

"The military has a long history of working with comedians and comedy writers," said Major Bobby. "Remember the Bay of Pigs? That was an Ernie Kovacs and Lenny Bruce thing. Look, plain and simple, humor is generated by a sudden, radical deviation from expected patterns of behavior in a situation characterized by incongruous or inappropriate elements, right? I see you comedy guys as extremely similar to the terrorists. The difference is that instead of using weapons of mass destruction to kill, you guys use jokes. I'm pissing my pants just thinking about some of your stuff," added the pee-stained Major.

With our national security at stake, nothing was considered out-of-bounds, some writers even breaking the rule of threes. Everyone pushed the envelope, except for Mel B., who actully got in the envelope. No joke was considered too provocative or graphic. Pipe was being laid from L.A. to Kabul, no matter how cheap, easy or done, they were evaluated equally. Exploding cigars, bio-germ squirting flowers, kick me signs and whoopee cushions loud enough to embarrass entire cities, double, triple and the never before attempted, quadruple entendres filled the room. Classics like Stooge-type fingers to the eyes, self-inflicting fists to the head and baked bean generated, round-the-campfire, gas attacks were simple yet not thought beyond terrorists' sinister possibilities. Spit-takes, Polish jokes, pratfalls, pies in the face and even the ever annoying, sitcom, see-it-coming-from-a-mile-away misdirection were all under consideration.

At one point a separate group of writers was sent out to come up with terrorist catchphrases that might evoke such reaction that they could be repeated infinitum. Some of those generated included, "Damn, this poi tastes poisonous," "Oh, Shoot," "Lookee there," "Don't you tell me that ain't no bomb, sucka" and, of course, the time-honored "Dyn-o-mite. Really, I have dynamite in my pants."

I never saw a comedy room so bent on cooperation. Everyone treated each other as peers, except for some bottom-rung term writers who, by Writers Guild guidelines, were belittled unmercifully. It was exhilarating. There were buttons placed on blows placed on call-backs that landed smack dab in the middle of an irony. And although only six of these meetings had been planned, Major Bobby said he expected the project to be picked up for the rest of the war.

Yet with all the exuberance of the creative process and the full year of health coverage, we all knew that we were writing for something more important.

We were writing for peace.

We were writing for freedom.

And if I might be so bold, to borrow from Brother Elwood Blues … "We were on a mission from God."

In the end I realized, it was not just any new terrorist plan they wanted from us. They wanted more than a conspiratorial idea so they might be one step ahead of the bad guys. What they needed was to make America laugh again. To show the bastards that they might have knocked out our buildings, but they couldn't knock out our humanity. And when we were told to get back to "normal," it would be up to us comedy writers to do our part, to help America laugh in between the tears.

And in between free meals, that's exactly what we did.

Okay, it's not as good as shopping or visiting Disneyland, but what is?

NOTE: The only hints of discontent came after moving to a studio office where there were a few battles over who would sit on the side of the couch nearest the fruit as well as brief fisticuffs over which restaurant we would order out from.

CHAPTER TWENTY-TWO

Being Drafted into Larry's Army

"What can I do?" I asked. "Why do you even trust me to do this? You don't really know me."

"That's why I had to send Lewis first," replied Larry. "I needed to check you out."

"Check me out?"

"Lewis has long had psychic abilities similar to Leonard Nimoy.'"

"From 'Star Trek?' You're talking about Nimoy's character, Dr. Spock?"

"No. Leonard Nimoy himself. His mind-melding at Hollywood parties was why there were Hollywood parties."

"But who would listen to me? I don't even really understand what the heck is happening. Why don't you ask someone like Ricky Gervais? He probably knows all about this and more. I mean, how many television writer/producers get to emcee the Oscars? If anyone has credibility here, it would be him."

"You obviously haven't heard."

"Heard what?"

"Gervais is dead."

Ricky Dene Gervais, the British import who brought his talents as well his hit series, *The Office*, a show about a Scranton, Pennsylvania stationary office, to the American airwaves. He also created the HBO series, *Extras*, a series about Hollywood extras. While his skill in creating titles that weren't perfectly obvious has been questionable, his deft talent in crafting killer comedies concepts and dialogue has never been in doubt.*41

I stood there, though with knees buckling I had to grab onto one of the naked Kissinger statues to keep from falling. Embarrassingly enough I had grabbed onto the statue's penis which gave hard evidence of Hank's enormous success with the ladies. Falling further I slipped onto Kissinger's scrotum. Oddly, I could feel only one testicle. Who knew?

"Groening, Brooks, Gervais and Kelly," I whimpered. "Has the world gone insane?"

"It's not Kelly. It's Kelley. With a second "e.""

"I'm sorry. That's what I meant. Kelley."

"Most importantly, this is insanity to those blind to the harsh reality. Cool and calculated to those who are in control."

"We're talking PHLEM again?"

Larry's oh-so-slick point-and-click annoyingly confirmed it.

"But why?"

Walking over to the wall he slid aside a small picture of a wall-safe revealing a small wall-safe behind it.

"Nixon made sure that every wall in America had a wall-safe, though many of them will never be found due to a gravitational schism fashioned by the White House Plumbers."

"Howard Hunt and James McCord?"

"No. Real, licensed plumbers from AAA Water, Sewage and Drainage Uncloggers. After the almost daily, severe clogs of the Oval Office toilets

41 *Continuing the once Steve Carell-lead "The Office" without Carell for the final two years of the show's existence has been labeled by former U.S National Security Advisor under President James Carter, Zbigniew Brzezinski, "insane." But other than that, and his larger-than-afterlife, Gervais was seemingly flawless. I mean, not counting "Dads."*

during the presidency of Lyndon Johnson, the selection of a professional on-site plumber has been the most important political appointment after Supreme Court nominee."

"Political appointment?"

"Congress needs to approve the choice. The more partisan the Congress, the more difficult it's been to settle on an acceptable plumber."

"A political battle over picking a White House plumber?"

"President Clinton went through a full eighteen months of congressional and toilet blockage before he was forced to name a plumber with a recess appointment."

Seven turns of the combination lock and a soft clank signaled that the safe was open.

"How do you know the combination?"

"Nixon, the fuck, thought he was some kind of cryptologist, so after losing the California gubernatorial race he came up with the sequence 38-2-54-64-63-34-2 as his own secret code."

"38-2-54-64-63-34-2? FU-C-KI-NG-ME-DI-A," I said incredulously as it was obvious that Nixon had depended on the simple, but classic, telephone letter-to-number paradigm. "Of course."

"Exactly," agreed Larry. "He used it as a safeguard for every locking device and undercover operation."

"But why would he use the same code all the time? Isn't the purpose of a secret code to make it especially difficult to determine each time you attempted to use it? Even if it wasn't for the fact that he used the simplest of codes to break, the repeated use of the same sequence makes no sense at all. I mean once you determine the code you could break into everything else he was trying to keep secret."

"Nixon had OCD. Being an obsessive-compulsive, he turned the White House lights on and off 38-2-54-64-63-34 and 2 times before leaving any room. It was the only series of numbers he could remember."

"Wow."

"The code was known inside the White House as 'The Holy Grail.'"

I almost choked on that one.

"Did you say 'Holy Grail?'"

"Um. No," Larry tittered nervously. "I meant, 'Pony Tail.'" They called it 'The Pony Tail.'"

Common mistake.

"I really gotta take a leak," said Larry, which I couldn't discern as a plea from a bursting bladder or an attempt to escape the conversation.

Larry tried to open the nearby restroom door. Locked.

"I'll be out in a minute," came a voice from inside.

"Shit."

"Larry, I get the whole PHLEM controlling the government. But why kill comedy writers?"

Visibly uncomfortable, but soldiering on, Larry pulled out a miniature projector from the wall-safe and placed it on the floor. He flicked a tiny switch on the back. Within short moments it projected a 3-D hologram image of a tiny person in a white gown.

"Princess Leia?" I guessed. Though no Star Wars fan, especially since I found out that the movie was, for the most part, fictional, the only white-draped hologram I ever knew of was Star War's Princess Leia, ava shulem, before drugs and alcohol turned her into a terrific film-writer.

"No," corrected Larry. "Mel Brooks."

I clearly hadn't looked that closely enough or it would have been obvious that it was not Carrie Fishers' Star War's character, Princess Leia, but the great screen and television writer, Mel Brooks. Brooks was the writer/producer of such gems as Get Smart, Blazing Saddles, High Anxiety, Twelve Chairs, The Producers (the original with Gene Wilder and Zero Mostel, not the film of the musical which was forbidden by the Writers

Guild to be seen by anyone who believed Brooks to be a swell writer). Brooks was also part of the legendary staff of Sid Caesar's 1950's television show, *Caesar's Hour*, which also included Neil Simon, Larry Gelbart, Mel Tolkin and Carl Reiner, among others.

"I didn't realize he was so short," I said.

Larry rolled his eyes. Literally. Right in front of where Brooks was speaking. I scooped them up, tossed them back to him and leaned in closer to hear Brooks' tiny voice: a cross between Carol Kane and a much shorter Carol Kane sucking on a balloon filled with helium.

"If you are watching this, I could very well be deceased," said Brooks. "In all likelihood, murdered by those who tired of my literary presence. And if I have been done away with, so probably have many more been eliminated by those who would not stand for the freedoms that true wit could bring."

"He's so damned short."

I just couldn't get over the fact that such a large talent came out of such a teeny body.

"Just listen," insisted Larry.

If Larry was anything, and he was many things, he was impatient.

"We were young and so was television," Brooks continued. "No one knew what they were doing so no one could tell us that they knew better, especially the suits at the network. Those who wore the suits knew even less. The result was that we could take creative risks and, while there were disappointments, the freedom we had resulted in many more successes. To wit, those successes produced countless hysterical ideas that audiences seemed to love. The ratings proved it. Consequently, both the writers and the audience became smarter. And that's when the shit hit the fan."

A slam-bang metaphor from one of the best.

"And just so there is no misunderstanding," continued Brooks, "that was no metaphor. It was an idea for a sketch that even Caesar thought was somewhat risky. To be perfectly honest, it was based on actual cow manure fertilizer being shot wildly around the set when we turned the stage fan on. While the bit was cut, it did lead to establishing at least two timeless metaphors: 'That's when the shit hit the fan' and 'throwing shit against the wall to see what sticks.' Let me tell you, plenty sticks and cleaning that shit off the walls took a lot more than a bottle of Mr. Clean, or heart be still, Mr. Clean himself."

Wow. Classic comedy AND parables. All we get today is "Talk to the hand" and "That's gonna leave a mark."

"And that's when it started," said a weeping Brooks. "They need to be stopped."

And with that startling, no metaphor-in-sight statement, the hologram dissolved. He was gone, gone before I got to ask him what a young Anne Bancroft was like. Honestly, an older Bancroft could send chills through me… "Are you trying to seduce me, Mrs. Robinson?"

"What is Brooks talking about?" I asked Larry.

"What *was* he talking about?" Larry corrected me. "He said he's probably dead. You need to use past tense."

An off the wall writer who is grammatically anal. Paradoxical. No wonder he and Lewis were such good friends.

"If you ever want to sell any of that crap you write, you better think about making it look professional."

He knows my work is crap. That means he's read my material. How cool.

"It's called being a pro."

"Yessir."

Guidance from a god. I'm living the dream.

"So, what was Brooks talking about?" I asked.

"Patience."

Patience, no patience. The guy is all over the place.

He reached into the wall safe.

"Look at this," he said pulling out a reel-to-reel tape canister. "Do you know what this is?"

"An old audio-tape case?"

"Eh. A very special old audio-tape case. It holds the missing minutes from the Nixon tapes."

"This is what Richard Lewis was talking about. He tried to tell me that there were more than eighteen minutes that were missing. Funny guy, but really…"

"Ye-e-eah… no. The tape was originally twenty-two minutes long."

"Again with the twenty-two minutes? Why have they always said there were eighteen minutes?"

"Why do women say they wear a size 6 shoe when their feet are a size 9?"

"I have no…"

"That's what they always want you to believe."

"Eighteen minutes. Twenty-two minutes. What does it matter? Great writers are dying because of Nixon's missing tapes?"

Larry looked around suspiciously, then, with visible sadness, nodded his head.

"And the missing twenty-two minutes are in that canister?" I asked.

"They were," said Larry. "We're not sure of anything anymore. The Protectors of PHLEM are careful. Very careful. They will not risk revealing the evidence that quality programming is being purposely verboten. And I know verboten sounds German, but if you want to be honest, it could also be Prussian. In any event, once that happens, they lose their power."

"What are you talking about?" I asked as I took hold of the canister and began to open it.

"NO!!!" cried out Larry.

But it was too late. A sizzling stream of smoke escaped from the canister, blinding me for the moment. Coughing and with fingers on fire, I dropped the now red-hot lid to the floor.

Larry used his always at-the-ready, solid gold, diamond-studded, nose-hair tweezers, which anyone who was anyone in Hollywood owned in an attempt to keep up with The Larry, to pick up the toasted canister. There was a reel inside, but no tape, melted or not, evident. Did it disintegrate due to some kind of CIA hush-hush Protective Elimination Device (PED)? Or was it what those with dyslexic acronym syndrome known as DEP?

On further examination, there was no evidence of tape, disintegrated or otherwise. The smoke had been just a special effect added to make the search for the missing eighteen – or twenty-two minutes all the more dramatic.

Larry *grinned* a weak smile at the finding ... or non-finding.

"And that, ladies and gentlemen," he announced, "is why they call them 'missing.'"

I turned over the canister and on the flip side was stamped, "CL 288" within a pentacle, the same inscription that seemed to be carved in blood on Larry's chest when I found him (sort of) dead.

"CL 288," I uttered quietly. "What the hell does that mean?"

"Everything. But I really have to go."

"You can't leave before you tell me what this is all about."

"I meant I have to go… to the can," he said with a palpable scowl.

He knocked on the bathroom door again, this time with greater urinary-provoked urgency.

"C'mon!"

"I'm hurrying as fast as I can," said the restroom occupant.

"For crissake. Do you know who I am?!"

Oh my god, Larry was trying to use his industry muscle to get some-one to wipe faster.

"I don't care who you are, you're not going to make my kidneys work any quicker than they are."

Man, wait till this guy finds out he's having a tete-e-tete with Larry David. Larry is going rip him a new one.

"Do you have a burning sensation?" asked Larry of the potty occu-pant. "You might have an infection?"

Huh? Larry's a doctor?

"It's not burning," said the guy inside. "Just a little hesitation."

"You could be dehydrated and not putting enough water into your system. Make sure you drink plenty of water. I recommend at least 7.8 glasses of water a day. Not a drop less. That way you should be expelling six to seven cups of urine."

"I already drink eight glasses."

"Try increasing to ten or twelve glasses."

"I only own eight glasses."

"How about salt? Do you use a lot of salt?

"I like salt."

"Avoid it. Salty foods can dehydrate you. Do you drink?

"On occasion. I mean I'm no alcoholic. I've gone to a couple meet-ings, but it's not for me."

"Alcohol can cause dehydration. I mean, I'm not telling you what to do. Tell you what. Instead of alcohol, try drinking one to two glasses of cranberry juice a day. Cranberry juice has cleansing properties for your urinary tract system. It can help aid in production and filtration. Keeps your system healthy which will help ward off infections that can cause decreased urine flow."

He cares. He really cares. This is the Larry David few know.

The door finally opened and to the surprise of both of us, no one was there. What the hell?

"Down here, schmucks," said the same voice we had heard from the restroom, but less muffled since there was no longer a door between us and the voice.

"Danny!" exclaimed Larry as he looked down.

It was Danny Woodburn, the little person who had played the character Mickey on *Seinfeld*. He was bearded and much taller than he appeared on the show.

"Hiya doin', Danny. This is a friend of mine, Steve."

His friend. Wow.

"Hi, Steve," Danny said as he extended his hand.

"Nice to meet you, Danny," I said as I shook his hand. "Hope you don't mind me saying this but you're like a foot taller than you looked on *Seinfeld*."

"I'm a professional actor. The character was supposed to be a foot shorter than I am, so that's the way I played it."

Actors, the illegitimate offspring of genius.

"What are you doing here?" asked Larry.

"I'm in the new Nixon musical, *Yes, He IS a Crook*. I play the part of Pat Nixon during the Watergate years."

"Ah. Hence the beard."

"Exactly."

"What are you guys doing here?"

"We're on a mission from God," said Larry out of the corner of his mouth.

"Which God?" asked Woodburn, a well-known authority of deities.

"All of them," responded Larry with great pride.

"Well, yeah. Gotta go," said Woodburn. "Director Kissinger don't stand for showing up late. Take care guys."

Woodburn left as Larry opened the bathroom and froze.

"Oy. What the hell was Danny eating at the Craft table?"

"What about CL 288?" I shouted as Larry closed the door behind him.

But he didn't hear me. Hey, he's only taking a leak. It's not like anything would deter Larry much more than a few minutes from giving me the critical information that could save humanity.

CHAPTER TWENTY-THREE

It Hits the Fan

O'Reilly paced in front of a framed photograph of a much younger O'Reilly, dressed in his favorite Elvis Presley impersonator-costume standing alongside a life-size poster of President Nixon in the Oval Office. He had already worn a deep trail into the BHCTF's plush Persian rug. It's one thing to make a multi-millionaire out of Al Franken, but having the alleged killer of some of the best television writers of all time escape, is another. And now Ricky Gervais. Not only would the continuing murderous scourge gut the reputation of the BHCTF, but it would also cut into Gervais's copious script output, though not seriously. Ricky had written so prodigiously that it would be years before all of his work could be consumed by an adoring public. I mean, I can't wait to start watching *Dads* which will probably be another understated and brilliant sitcom by Gervais.

O'Reilly was taking it personally. He had never lost a man before, 'cepting for his messy public break-up with former domestic partner, the late Andy Rooney, over Rooney's prejudicial comments blasting Mel Gibson's "Christ" film. Not the theatrically released "Passion of the Christ" blockbuster, but the straight-to-video, animated "Passion of the Christ Kid," which examined the twelve-year old Jesus's fascination with street basketball. Playing for the Jerusalem Junior Disciples, the young Christ averaged a triple-double during the Roman army's strike-shortened season.

"Cancel all vacations and leaves," screamed O'Reilly to Frank Rich, part time New York Times theater/film reviewer and O'Reilly's second in command. "I want every man, woman and Ann Coulter you can dig up at BHCTF on this case. And then after that, go outside in your underwear and hop on one leg while you scream like a rooster."

It wasn't the first nor far from the last time O'Reilly would send Rich out to perform ignominious, seemingly meaningless, tasks.

O'Reilly ruminated over his surreptitious history with Rich. A history he dare not reveal to friend nor foe and especially to those who ran the BHCTF.

As young man, O'Reilly had been a street urchin on the sanguine mean streets and cul de sacs of Studio City, California. Wise to the way of the streets, anyone who needed anything in the *studio hood* had to go through O'Reilly. It was the mid-sixties and O'Reilly had been dealing tri-uranium octoxide for the nuclear warhead buildup in North Hollywood High's impending hostilities with crosstown rival, Encino Prep. O'Reilly, who even back then was always looking out for *you*, saw an opportunity for doubling and tripling his business by not only selling out to the highest bidder, but also to the second, third and fourth highest bidder. As a double, triple and quadruple agent, Bill was not only receiving more cash and illicit massages than he would ever be able to turn in for valuable gifts and light appliances, but he also caught the eye of the CIA who had been looking to place a young agent in one of their most feared hotbeds of celebrity terrorism: "The Valley."

In coordination with the CIA, Secretary of Defense, Robert McNamara, had erroneously thought the Valley would make the perfect beachhead for U.S. Marines readying for the impending covert action into Viet Nam. Only later would McNamara admit that this geographic faux pas would be the first of many more to come in the un-fucking-believable, botched, non-declared war effort.[*42]

---

42 *Unfortunately, the "Valley" McNamara had wanted to escalate the war from was in the Mai Kong Delta "Valley" area of Viet Nam, not the Los Angeles area San Fernando one.*

When the CIA attempted to make the phone call to O'Reilly, they misconnected – a commonplace bit of confusion in the mid-sixties due to Bell Telephone monopoly's *bottom-line trumps intellect* cost-cutting tact of assigning the same phone number to every Valley home. With phones ringing simultaneously and continuously all over the Valley, most of Bell's customers had given up answering ... except for the persevering Frank Rich.

Rich had never actually received a phone call meant for him but was nevertheless the type of kid who never gave up hope. He ended up receiving the call as well as the job meant for O'Reilly. O'Reilly who had always had a dream to become a James Bond-like secret agent, never forgave Rich, nor revealed to him that he had taken from O'Reilly the one desire he never realized.

O'Reilly pulled out his "Just Because It's Personal or Without Merit Doesn't Mean You Can't Go Public" list. He ran a finger down the names: Franken, Rooney, Clinton, Clinton, Ludacris, Most Everyone in Hollywood, Rich. Stopping at "Rich," he placed a check mark, one of some twenty that he had previously marked next to that name.

As he folded his list of well-considered and well-checked *betrayers*, most obvious was the one name that had yet to receive a single check mark.

Larry David.

Right below Larry was a name that would have seemed the last name you would expect O'Reilly to care about.

Steve Young.

Not the football player who had once dated Marie Osmond, nor the David Letterman writer I would constantly receive WGA residuals from (who did not date Marie Osmond, that I know of), but me, who also never dated Marie Osmond [*43], that I know of.

Not that it plays any part of the story, but Marie really keeps herself in tiptop shape. I never saw her when she tended to blow up, not as

43 *When I was first introduced to Marie she actually said, "I used to date you."*

much as Kirstie Alley did, but damnit, you have to give it to both of them, they cut fine figures when they worked at it. Having spent time with both, they even looked good close up. Really, the only difference was that Kirstie never told me she dated me.

CHAPTER TWENTY-FOUR

Ztivo

The filthy motel room was beginning to take on the rich flavor of its occupant's unwashed condition. As was his wont, Ztivo sat in the middle of the floor, his body stained deeply from the literary and literal blood of his victims.

Not one to let go of past injustice, nor dirt buildup, Ztivo went over, as he did every evening, the inequity of it all. His sing-song litany of blame echoed like a Hollywood Gregorian Chant.

"Damn Geffen. Damn Eisner. Damn New York Times. Damn *Gay Mafia*. Damn everyone but me. Damn Hollywood Reporter and damn Variety. Oh, wait, Variety is kind of okay."

Alright, the chant had some rough edges, but Ztivo wasn't looking for a Grammy. He was just laying out the list of those he deemed responsible for his slide downhill.

There was plenty more on his blame inventory but absolutely no accountability on his part. With the counsel of PHLEM and its notorious Master, Ztivo was ready and able to take what he felt was just and due retaliation. He hadn't been able to pick and choose his own victims but wiping out those whose words were respected by the mainstream media did hold a certain amount of gratification. Almost sexual. So much so, Ztivo called in a refill of his Cialis RX and started filling the water in his side-by-side bathtubs.

Previously he had taken it on his own to eradicate writer/producer/ actor Tyler Perry but was severely chastised by the Master.

"I said *respected* writers!" the Master admonished Ztivo.

Unbeknownst to Ztivo, Perry was, in reality, an android that could be easily replaced by another programmed Perry-android that would replicate the same mind-numbing, vanilla formula that not Perry, but the Masters, had created to facilitate their diabolical plan.

Ztivo's murmured chants were interrupted by the phone. It was the Master.

"Were you chanting?" asked the Master knowing full well the answer.

"Yes, Master."

"Did you remember to blame Geffen?"

"Yes, Yes I did," Ztivo declared, proud to have pleased the Master.

"What about Eisner?"

"Indeed. Fucker"

"Good. He never did give you near enough the golden parachute you deserved, you know."*[44]

"Yes, I know," Ztivo agreed as he always did when anyone conceded that he had been screwed royally by life.

"We have another task for you."

Just the slightest hint of a smile grew on Ztivo. Next to firing a lowly CAA agent trainee, Ztivo liked nothing better than to *do* a successful industry creator. Or is it *doon*?

44 *Ztivo had received a severance package from the head of a child's studio for something over $100 million, depending on the worth of the studio stock which hinged on if Comcast was in the process of buying the studio or not.*

CHAPTER TWENTY-FIVE

Not Again

Larry was taking a long time in the rest room, long even for his age.

"Larry," I whispered with a bit more than a whisper.

Nothing.

"Aren't you finished yet?"

Even more nothing.

"Larry," I said with more alarm. "Are you okay?"

Nothing was getting louder by the second.

This was too much.

"Larry, if you don't answer me right now, I will knock down that door."

Did you hear that? Me, one of the least accomplished of the show biz ilk, demanding one of the most successful to do what I wanted him to. Even more so, I was threatening to do something that I had seen in the movies plenty of times as well as twenty-five times a day *Cops* was on TV. And I threatened it, knowing that in real life, anything short of a balsa wood door would break my shoulder before I could budge it, let alone break it down. Still, anything I could do that might endear me to Larry.

I'd give it a shot.

I steadied myself about twenty feet from the door, getting down in a three-point halfback stance that I had learned during my years at good old Home Depot College of Gutter and Rain Spout Installation. I wasn't on the team. I just watched enough football on TV while I was supposed to be studying so that I knew well which three points were supposed to be on the ground.

"Hut one. Hut two. Hut…"

I was flying on my way towards the door, already feeling the bone-breaking pain I was about to endure. Here it comes…

Of course, this is the point that in most comedies the door would open and I would fly through and into the wall on the other side. Nope.

BAM.

Much to my surprise… I knocked down the door. Shoulder intact. Door made of balsa. Who knew?

"Larry?"

I got up and warily opened the room's single toilet stall door. Other than the rich aroma of a combination of recent public restroom fecal and urine evidence, the stall was empty.

Larry was nowhere to be found. The restroom window was open, which I could tell by the nearby curtains flapping in the air. Other than in film, especially animation, I rarely see curtains over public restroom bathroom windows. But in this case, they were necessary to determine an open window through which someone probably exited.

It wasn't the largest window in the world, even though I couldn't tell you how big the largest window in the world was. Tell you what, if you wanted to believe the Columbus Window Cleaning Company website, it would be the window at the Notre Dame Cathedral in Paris that had a diameter reaching over thirty-nine feet. The window in the bathroom was smaller than that. This was a casement (crank) window that could create a larger opening, versus, say, a double- hung window which would only provide something less than half the opening of a casement. It's not something that everyone would be aware of but if you saw Hitchcock's *Rear Window*, which depicted a double-casement window (two casement windows together) you would see what propelled me into what was to become a life-long fascination with windows and the openings they provide.

'Course the biggest conundrum was that we were in the basement. How many windows that size have you ever seen in a basement? Of course, if you want to get a wide look at the beautiful scenery provided by a window facing a wall, it was perfect. I peeked out and we were at least five floors up. A fifth-floor basement? Something wasn't making any sense. Nothing made any sense. But this wasn't a time for logic. It was time for the next paragraph.

Most glaring were the letters and numbers written on the window-sill – CL288 – the same inscription carved into LD's hologrammed torso when I found what I thought to be him in his bed. A closer inspection revealed the inscription was written IN BLOOD! Wait a minute. Was this…? Yes it was. This was the blood of Larry David. No deoxyribonucleic acid[*45] test necessary here. Since the death of the esteemed Don Knotts, there could be no other person with the visible anxiety level of this blood. If his blood had wings, they would be a hummingbird's. You could actually hear the blood humming. I think it was "Tie a Yellow Ribbon ('Round the Old Oak Tree)." Who could forget the venerable Dawn?

I scooped up the blood, placing it into the vial I always kept handy to collect questionable, potentially bacteria-laden evidence.

"You're traveling through another dimension, a dimension not only of sight and sound but of mind," said Rod Serling. "Into a wondrous land whose boundaries are that of imagination. Next stop, the Cell Phone Zone."

My cool ringtone continues to throw me for a loop even though I was the one who downloaded it. I'm pretty sure it wasn't the actual Rod Serling, venerable creator and on-air host of *Twilight Zone*, maybe the most terrifying television show to air until the chilling debut of *The Big Bang Theory*, which for the life of me I don't get why people say it's meant for

---

45 *Deoxyribonucleic acid is sometimes referred to as "DNA," by the severely syllable-challenged.*

smart people. I mean, I love Chuck Lorre as a person, but using scientific or technical terms doesn't make a joke clever. It just makes the references less pronounceable. Half of former comedian Dennis Miller's references are so obscure that Wikipedia has no reference to them. Obscure can be funny, but only when the joke is funny.

Then again, Serling seemed to know a lot of stuff that you would never figure anyone in the sixties could have known, so maybe he did record it figuring that one day we'd have access to ringtones we could download. Or, it could have been some hack comic impressionist. They need to make money too. You never know.

I checked my cell phone screen. "O'Reilly, Bill."

Detective O'Reilly. My cell phone number was unlisted. How could a police detective who knew NSA department heads personally and Verizon operators intimately ever get a hold of my cell phone number, I thought ironically.

"Steve Young," came a familiar voice from a bullhorn outside the window. "This is Detective O'Reilly from the Beverly Hills Celebrity Task Force. Come out with your hands up."

Shit. How did he...? What is the acronym for "Oh my God?" Damn. Oh, my God. Right. OMG! He's tracking me through my cell phone. I thought long and hard, but sex wasn't helping at all. Then it hit me.

I threw my phone in the toilet and flushed... twice. You never want to chance a clog.

"We know you're in there!" blared O'Reilly, no longer using the bull-horn as his voice was louder without it.

I wanted to yell, "Come in and get me, copper," with a rich Jimmy Cagney inflection, but in the confusion, I delivered the line much more like Jimmy Stewart, a stammer which almost no one over three feet away could hear.

O'Reilly checked his tracking device then turned to second in command, Frank Rich.

"Great Sid Caesar's Ghost! He's trying to escape through the toilet."

O'Reilly, Rich and the rest of the BHCTF rushed into the building.

I thought fast, but as fast as I thought, I thought of nothing. A catch-22 for sure. I slowed my thinking process just a bit.

But where could I escape? I heard the BHCTF running towards the restroom door.

I glanced at the toilet. A possible exit? No. Too obvious.

I'm supposed to be a writer. I create. At my best I generate serious conflict – even in comedy – then use my creativity to surprise the audience with a unique resolution. I needed to find out what happened to Larry and at the same time I needed to escape so I didn't end up behind bars for murder. Add to that, this crazy, supposed years-long conspiracy to squash quality television. So…

Run away!*[46]

The only exit seemed to be the window. It was at this time that all logic went out the … window. A so-called *10,000 year storm* hit, where atmospheric and esoteric conditions collided perfectly so that all cognitive receptors reversed simultaneously. It resulted in the basement no longer sitting on the bottom of the building as much as on the top floor.

Crazy, huh?

I crawled out the window and onto a six-inch ledge. I had watched many film and television scenes where a character had attempted to escape through a window and onto a narrow ledge. Due to my acrophobia, I could barely watch those film scenes without shitting my pants. Unfortunately, not much difference in real life.

46 *Thank you, Monty Python and Bertie, the rabid rabbit.*

With the odor seeping up along with a severe case of dazed and confused, I caught sight of a fast-approaching tandem axle tractor on the street below hauling a 45' open trailer full of large, foam, flowered pillows.

Convoluted? Sure. But when you're stuck on a ledge five stories above the street you don't reject lifesaving works of fiction.

As the BHCTF rushed into the bathroom, I realized I had no choice.

I jumped.

Regrettably, the soft, fluffy pillow-laden tractor had made a quick turn at the corner before my building leaving a very hard-top Prius racing to the spot directly under my rapidly approaching body. With eyes and sphincter closed tight, I prepared for my oncoming splatter.

And… scene.

CHAPTER TWENTY-SIX

Contrived, Thy Name Be Me

Huh?

My landing was far softer than I had anticipated.

Luckily, the hard-top Prius sedan was actually a hard-top convertible that had opened its top just as I dropped into the back seat, a back seat packed with fluff sitcom scripts.

"Um. Sorry," I apologized to the driver. "I was on the ledge of a building trying to get away from these guys who think I murdered this guy who I not only didn't murder but who is still, in fact, alive that… Ah, forget it. It's far too complicated to explain. I mean, if you're really interested, I could give you the central beats…"

SCREECH!

I was launched toute de suite into the windshield.

"Get out!"

"I'm sorry, I didn't mean to just drop in to…"

"I don't care," the driver interrupted. "I already can't stand your incessant whining."

"Incessant? You want to hear incessant? Just give me and couple hours and…"

Holy crap!

"Elaine Benes?!"

"Julia Dreyfus, please," she said with a tight smirk.

"Wow! I can't believe…"

"Just get out."

"But how…? What? Why? As well as where, when and who?"

Yes, I was stealing from Kipling…

> *I keep six honest serving-men*
>
> *(They taught me all I knew);*
>
> *Their names are What and Why and When*
>
> *And How and Where and Who.*

Not exactly "The Charge of the Light Brigade," but really, what is?

"Out… now. Now!" exclaimed Juila.

Perhaps a more empathetic approach.

"Your head is much smaller than on TV," I said, trying to calm the anxiety she felt during the *Seinfeld* episode where she thought her head was too large.

"Fuck you," she noted as she peeled out.

"I love your work!" I shouted at the rapidly departing Prius.

As Dreyfus drove out of sight, I could barely see the finger she stationed just outside the driver-side window.

I really do love her work. I bet she keeps her house neat as pin. Not just stacking up things but putting them away in a well-ordered fashion. In any event, her head is enormous.

I stood alone on the quiet, palm tree-lined street, dotted with large, opulent homes all protected by massive gates. Where was I? If I didn't know better*[47], I would have thought that I was in a very expensive Beverly

---

47 *"If I didn't know better…" just seems to be one of those filler phrases that adds absolutely nothing to the conversation, say like, "absolutely nothing" when "nothing" itself clearly denotes something absolute, thereby making the use of the adjective "absolutely," absolutely unnecessary.*

Hills-adjacent neighborhood. So adjacent was this neighborhood that it may have been Beverly Hills itself.

I found a soft section of grass and sat down leaning against a psalm*[48] tree. What the hell had I gotten myself into? I just wanted to pick up on a lousy interview and I ended up being pursued by the police for a string of murders. Questions were racing through my mind like a spoiled pint of Danon Yogurt careening towards a speedy exit from my colon.

Who was behind the killings? Or who WERE behind the killings? I couldn't be sure of the number of perpetrators. And why were they killing? Or why was he, she or they killing? Damn those night school gender grammar courses. Where did Larry disappear to? And YES, it is okay now to end a sentence with a preposition… over.*[49]

About the only question I didn't have was, "Who left the dogs out?" That had become abundantly clear from my earlier investigative story on Mr. Charles Montgomery Burns who seemed to have a proclivity for "releasing the hounds" on innocent children and other living things. Turns out it was former Credibility Gap*[50] member, Harry Shearer who, unbeknownst to Burns, was spraying kibble-nitrate on unsuspecting visitors to the Burns' mansion so that whenever the door was opened, the dogs did what hungry dogs do when they're let out. In addition, it was confirmed years later that it had not been Burns himself who requested the hounds to be released but Shearer who had voiced-over Burns, a miserable discontent, who had actually said, "Release the clowns." Who knows what could have been worse.

---

48 *Only later did I find that the bark of this particular psalm tree was used by early 20th century, Los Angeles hymnists to humanize Beverly Hills residents through biblical tree psalms.*

49 *Though varied as to the source and the exact phrasing, Winston Churchill, in response to an editor who told him that he had to stop ending sentences with prepositions, Churchill was to have said, "Ending sentences with a preposition is something up with which I will not put. BAM!*

50 *Brilliant, groundbreaking, satirical radio group: Shearer, David Landers (Squiggy), Michael McKeon (Lenny), sometimes Christopher Guest and Albert Brooks, all started by Lew Irwin.*

I pulled the blood vial from my pocket and rolled it around in my hand. What did CL288 mean? I pondered the cryptic possibilities. C is the third letter in the alphabet most exploited by Hollywood writers. Mostly a hard C. It has been used a great deal to indicate a person one might see as a… um, you know… the c-word. I just can't write it. Christ, C could mean so many things. CL has far more specific likelihoods. It stands for chlorine as a chemical element. As a roman numeral it signifies the number 150. Mercedes-Benz has a CL-Class automobile. Of course, most people think of CL as the abbreviation for light crude oil on the New York Mercantile Exchange.

I was lost. Nothing made sense.

I stood up, not knowing where I should go next, only sensing that staying in one place merely narrowed my pursuers' options of finding me.

Turning around I found that I was standing in front of a humongous, Solid Gold gate. Not that the gate was made of gold, but that there were images of dancers from the 1980's *Solid Gold* television series about the corners of each gate. And wouldn't you know it, looking closer I found that it was also manufactured from a rich gold that to the metallurgy-challenged eye, looked pretty damn solid.

In the middle of the gates were the initials…

CL

The design may seem large on the page but, in fact, it was the actual size of the letters on the gate. Not all that large.

Just then the great gates began to slowly creak open to reveal behind them an attractive Jewish writer/producer… the extremely prodigious Chuck Lorre (or Charles Levine for his pre-success family members) standing there between two large well-tanned, armed bodyguards. If I didn't already know that the WWE was holding its annual steroid fuck and suck retreat that every present former champion, including Bruno Sammartino, Ed "Strangler" Lewis and Donnie Osmond, was mandated to attend, I would have thought Lorre was being guarded by Hulk Hogan and The Rock.

Lorre was the creator of over 957 original sitcoms, give or take a couple hundred. Chuck was so prolific that he was said to have once written and sold fifteen separate series in one 24-hour period, three of which had been written in his sleep. He created *Dharma & Gregg, Cybill, Two and a Half Men, The Big Bang Theory, Someone and Molly, Momma, Dadda, One of My Sisters, The Kids, The Kids Next Door, Can't Think What I Should Call This One*" and 37 more since last week. So fertile was his sitcom-churning brain, lesser producers would go through his trash for the pages Chuck threw away (because he saw them as unintelligible) and turned them into their own shows. Hence the sauce-stained script pages found their way into the *brilliant* Wayans Brothers, *Homeboys in Outer Space* masterwork.

His initials on the gate epitomized who this great man was – letters that may have appeared large on the page, but not on the gate. It was the mark of a man whose impact on the page has been larger than life, but whose success didn't necessarily need to be shoved down lesser writers' throats. That, my friends, is the badge of a true gentleman. Being worth over a half a billion will do that for you.

"Come in, Steve," Lorre said with a hefty chortle.*[51] "I've been expecting you."

Years before I had interviewed Lorre for an industry cover story for "Written Schmitten Magazine" and he still remembered me. What an up.

I started to walk in.

"Hold it there," said Lorre. "Hulk, Rock… check him out." (See what I did there)

---

51 *Sadly, "chortle" has gone the way of "chuckle,""snicker" and "titter," and other delightful references to light, but appreciative laughter. The dwindling usage of these words may be traced to today's hipsters who think they're so cool by never chortling and such. I for one will not let these words go the way of the duel-genital sea monkey. I beseech you, when an opportunity emerges, don't just smile. Damn these societal mores killing off so many lost or soon-to-be lost words.*

The two behemoths padded me down for three minutes taking generous liberties when inspecting my more sensitive areas.

"Hey! Do you really need to fondle me as part of your inspection?"

"Nah," said a giggling Hulk. "The inspection ended over two minutes ago."

Hulk and Rock high-fived as Lorre waved me in.

As we walked through the luscious gardens, strewn with hundred dollar bills and dreadful reviews of a Charlie Sheen stage show, *Am I Nuts or Just Rich?* he had attempted to perform without concept, story or script. Lorre seemed at peace. He stopped in front of a life-sized statue of Rosanne Barr firing Cybill Shepherd.

"Steve, let me ask you something."

"Sure, Charlie. Anything."

"There have been many wars in the name of God," said Charlie stating the obvious.

"I guess."

Other than reading in depth about the onset of TV commercials playing louder than regular programming, I'm not much of a history buff so I relied solely on the probability that Chuck knew what he was talking about. But that's when he hit me with one of those unanswerable questions. I mean it's answerable, but answerable only if you open your mouth and say words.

"Whose side has God been on?"

CHAPTER TWENTY-SEVEN

God. Discuss.

"Wow," I said, truly taken aback. "What a great question."

"Do you have an answer?"

I tried to gather my thoughts. My answer could very well merit a writing position on one of the fifteen shows Chuck would premiere the following week. My idea had to be smart yet comprehensible to a wide demographic.

"I guess it depends on the war."

"You mean that God sits on his throne and decides which of his children, all of whom he created in his image, he would side with?"

Think Steve. Maybe Costco is still hiring. Free bulk snacks. Great health benefits, even for same sex couples.

"I mean, maybe it hinges on what you're fighting over," I mused.

"Go on…."

"Well, if we're talking about a sports event, I guess I would want God to be on the side of the team I'd want to win."

"You mean each person gets to choose which side God should be on? We control God?"

"Well, I guess…"

"So, since there are people behind both teams, other than a tie, God is not only on the side of the team that wins, but He's also on the side of the team that loses?"

"Yeah, but He's God. He could switch from the team that's losing to the winning side just before the end of the game. I don't want to even consider His position in the possibility of overtime or a tie."

"So, God is a flip-flopper."

"I mean he's not running for political office. He's God."

"Let's get back to my original question concerning war. Real war. War where real people suffer and die."

"You're talking about where Americans die, right? Not those who look different than us or that you read about on the Internet."

Lorre might be a nice guy, but it was obvious that he was losing patience.

"During the Crusades, the Catholic Church fought and slaughtered people in an effort to stop the spread of Islam. Hitler attempted to annihilate the Jews in part to *purify* his country and race. There are terrorists today who, fighting in the name of a god, rationalize the propriety of innocent children dying and chopping off the heads of innocents.

"In war," Lorre asked sternly, "whose side is God on?"

"It's obvious that God wouldn't be on the side of those assholes. He'd be on the side of the good guys."

"You mean the good guys who dropped atomic bombs on Hiroshima and Nagasaki?"

"Well…"

"Or do you mean those who rationalize the death of innocents due to the unavoidable inconvenience of 'collateral damage?'"

"Okay. I get it. Maybe He stays out of war altogether," I said without much conviction.

"You're saying that God doesn't have a hand in how things turn out when life and death are involved?"

We reached his front door. Chuck placed his substantial hand – the writing one – on my shoulder.

"Steve. What if God's not on anyone's side?"

"What do you mean? You're the one who asked me whose side God is on?"

"Yes, I did," said Lorre. "And I asked it hoping that you would look at all possibilities, not just a thoughtless either/or."

I thought hard. Either/or was one of my favorite ways of deciding things. Thinking further than those two possibilities made my head hurt. If God wasn't on one side nor was he on both sides where was he? Christ. I'm being hunted down like some homicidal monster and this guy is giving me a Philosophy 101 test. Okay. Time to reach into my sack of bullshit.

"Well, if God exists and He can't be on one side or the other or on both sides at the same time, perhaps – and I'm just spit-balling here – it's not whose side God is on but who is on the side of God?"

The smile nearly broke Lorre's face.

"So then, it's up to us?" Chuck asked.

"I guess."

"We're given the ability to make a choice," said Chuck. "What some might call 'free will.'"

"You know," I chuckled. "Up until you said, 'free will,' I never realized how close that was to *Free Willy*."

"What?"

"The movie, *Free Willy*. I wonder if they named the whale, 'Willy,' so that when he is freed it's not only him being set free but it's also a metaphor for our need to have free will to truly be free."

"Okay, but…"

"Really, if we're honest and that's what they were trying to do, y'gotta admit it's pretty contrived. I never saw the whole movie, but I saw enough of the trailer that I got the idea. You might as well have someone in the kitchen slicing a piece of cheese and call the movie, *Who Cut the Cheese*. Of course you'd want to insert some adage for a gaseous smell, but no matter, *Free Willy* is just the type of on-the-money messaging that has 'trying too hard' written all over it."

"Are you finished?"

"Yeah. I guess. Except… was that whale trained for the film and if so, wouldn't that be the antithesis of the film's spirit?"

Chuck grabbed me by my biceps and pinned me against the wall with what I could only guess would be about the same rage he felt for Cybill Shepherd when she fired him from *Cybill*, a show that Chuck had created.

He was quite an intellect, which made the powerful force of his shove all the more surprising.

"You done?"

It was all I could do to coax a weak nod. He released me leaving indentations so deep in my biceps that for years later they would whistle whenever I walked through a brisk wind.

"What if I were to tell you that there are powerful people whose sole function was to take away your free will, your free will to make a choice, any choice?"

"Geesh. Lewis, David, now you."

"And not only are they taking away our free will, they're also doing it for their own selfish profit and power."

"To tell you the truth, this whole thing is starting to sound like one of your closing credit vanity cards."*[52]

---

52 *Vanity cards are displayed used at the end of a program's credits to brand the production company. For Chuck Lorre they became a method to philosophize on almost anything, including Charlie Sheen.*

"HOLY SHIT," I thought to myself in capital letters.

C-L-2-8-8.

CL288 was a Chuck Lorre Vanity card!

Chuck smiled like he had read my mind, pulled a folded manila envelope from his pocket and handed it to me.

"You might want to read what's inside here."

He opened the door to his mansion.

"Come on, Steve. The lawn has ears."

BAM!

CHAPTER TWENTY-EIGHT

Clean Up, Aisle IIIch

You know what it's like when you're having a conversation with someone and just then his head explodes?

Well, it's not one of those times that you prepare yourself for. Really, I don't know if there's an appropriate response that reflects the horror of the moment.

"Say what?!" gives you at least a moment to gather your thoughts, but even then, a recently detonated head doesn't leave much possibility for a rationale response. With charred and bloodied skin, teeth and brain fragments splattered all about you, it's pretty much all you can do to not go into shock.

"Holy fuck!"

Yep. That's pretty much the best I could do at that moment I watched Chuck Lorre's head get blowed up real good.

So odd that for most of my career I had wished that something from someone with the cache of Chuck would rub off on me. Here, literally, was Chuck not only rubbing off on me but some parts were solidly fusing to my parts.

Even more frightening was that Chuck's body, shoulders on down, remained upright for what seemed like a half-hour (more like twenty-two minutes if you don't include commercials). Finally he, or it, fell against me. That's something that should give one pause. At one point, with body parts

ejecting from one another at rapid speed, does the body begin to dehu-
manize? It's not so much a philosophical matter as much as a grammatical
one: "he" versus "it." Improperly assigning pronouns doesn't necessarily
kill a sentence but it can be distracting, especially when you are under
attack from some unknown killing machine.

With my body quivering at the speed of the wings of a hummingbird
with Parkinson's, I don't know how I was able to walk let alone sync my
body into *runaway* mode. I jumped over Chuck's headless body noticing
that his left-hand continued writing, writing about ten pages into a new
sitcom script. More amazingly, Chuck was right-handed.

Talk about perseverance.

I started (tried) to run, but my feet wouldn't comply. A bullet whizzed
near enough to my nose that I could smell the cold steel speeding by. It had
a hazelnut fragrance neatly cut by a sugar substitute. Not a name variety,
say like Sweet & Low, but a bulk store brand. If memory serves, Suite n
Sade'.

A bullet shot by my left ear nearly kissing (no tongue) the edge of my
lobe. Another bullet shot by my other ear. If you averaged out the two shots
I would have been shot twice, kill-shots, dead-center forehead. Luckily
math played no part.

I was still unharmed, but before I had time to celebrate, I was struck
hard on the top of my head.

I had been hit!

My mind started to race. This was it. A single bullet to my head and I
was about to meet my maker. Not my mom nor my dad. At best they were
conduits through which my maker, as I assumed to be God, had juiced my
parents enough one night to help create me in His image, or so someone
who once watched the 700 Club had told me. I am nowhere near religious
but at this point making some last second conversion from agnostic to fun-
damentalist believer made perfect sense.

My life began to pass in front of my eyes. I thought of all I had accomplished but that was quickly replaced by all that I hadn't. Worse were the *almosts*, the thoughts of those things I was about to do but at the last moment decided not to do because I was too terrified, unprepared or incapable of reaching some goal that might have made my life worthwhile… in the least tolerable.

Whew. This dying thing was becoming a busy, multi-tasking effort. Distracted, I couldn't keep my mind on dying. I was too busy thinking of the life I had wasted. My existence had been counterproductive. Negative, at best. I really should have thought ahead. You know, like those people in commercials who had put money aside so that they wouldn't have to work as a limousine driver into their sixties and seventies. I have nothing against chauffeurs, just me having to be one to pay the rent. Notice I didn't say mortgage? That would have meant I had somehow managed to save enough money to afford a down payment on a house of my own.

Everything I pursued had to be so fucking immediate and self-centered. And what about the fact that I was just shot? Talk about no sense of priority. Shot in the head and I'm bemoaning my lack of a home loan. For crissakes, what is the sense of rehashing something I did or didn't do twenty or more years ago? Especially now, a *very close to dying* now. It is so unfair to my last moments on earth. My whole approach to dying seemed unfocused, just like the rest of my life.

Blood poured from my head wound. Fortuitously, and thank Godiously, I realized for the first time, it wasn't from a bullet wound.

I looked up just as a metal bar was making its way, about to hit my head… again. I grabbed what was the bottom rung of a chained ladder dangling from a circling helicopter. I could barely make out someone in the helicopter waving at me to grab onto the ladder.

It wasn't like there was another choice. I wrapped both hands around the bottom rung and hung on for dear life as the ladder was reeled up into the helicopter.

I ran my hand though my hair and felt a thick goo, very similar to what blood might feel like. What a lot of blood would feel like if, in fact, it was blood... which it was. It was coming from what felt like a slight scratch. I was always what some people call a "bleeder." Not exactly a hemophiliac but it kept me from shooting heroin because the mess that would spill from my veins would be insufferable. Cleaning up my blood spill would be of far more concern than would be the enjoyment of my drug high. That, in itself, demonstrated either a serious lack of any ability to experience pleasure or I was getting piss-poor heroin from my dealer, Dukey... if I had a dealer... and his name was Dukey.

Fuck you, Dukey. You fictional low life.

I'm not one for heights. Sitting on a bar stool without a seatbelt sends tremors through my legs. As I was being pulled up, I looked down to see a manically smiling Michael Ztivo taking dead aim at my rapidly shrinking testicles, embedding themselves deeper and deeper into the shelter of my inner scrotum.

I could almost hear the clatter of the bullet rolling into the magnum's chamber. Ztivo slowly, carefully pulled back on the trigger making sure not to vibrate the crosshairs on his site one iota off my pubic hairs. And...

Click.

More of a... clunk.

Pistol jammed.

JAMMED PISTOL!

God damn! What luck. Someone is looking out for me. Now that I wasn't dead, at least for that split second, I knew things were going to change for the good. Except, I had no idea how. Still, not being dead... it's a start.

Ztivo threw it towards me and let out a wounded roar. A giant, wounded giraffe roar. Giraffes don't make sounds, right? Because Ztivo made no sound, just a wide-opened mouth where a roar could have wailed through but didn't.

Moments later I found myself being helped though the helicopter's open hatch by no other than… Larry David.

"Jesus Christ, Larry. What the hell is happening?!"

"Relax. I'll explain it as soon as you take a couple deep breaths."

He was right. I was hyperventilating.

"Who's piloting this thing?"

And from the cockpit came the comforting, "Hiya, doin.'"

In the pilot's seat, none other than the dashing, black-clad, Richard Lewis, complete with solid-charcoal goggles and pullover cap with the flaming initials, D.L. embroidered across the brim."

"I didn't know you could fly one of these things."

"I can't, but when the future of civilization is at risk, you do what you have to do."

"But, if I'm not mistaken, this is a UH-72A Lakota Light Utility Helicopter with electro-optical/infrared sensor, enhanced cockpit screens, high power illumination system, analog-digital data downlink capability and GPS-enhanced moving map displays. You don't figure how to pilot one of these beauties without a good five hundred hours of intense training."

"My dentist, Ben Laden, was a former pilot during Nam," said Lewis. "His waiting room was full of military publications. Captain Dr. Laden's penchant for running late on his appointments gave me more than enough time to run through every *Hell's Helicopters*, *Whirlybird Illustrated* and *Killing Fly Birds* magazine."

"Nice," I said without necessarily believing it was nice as much as I knew Lewis would be pleased if I thought it was.

"'The copter came with this," said Lewis as he unfolded a large white poster-sized sheet illustrating an eight-step, quick-start instructions for the UH-72A.

I had always wondered what took technology companies so long to simplify their instructions so that people without engineering degrees would know you had to plug in an electrical unit before a current would run through it.

"Nice, Dick."

Just then, the copter dipped down and to the right leaving my stomach about two hundred feet above my waist.

"Fuck," yelled Lewis. "Still getting used to wind currents. Look at me, using terms like 'wind currents.' Like I'm some kind of experienced flyer person."

"Flyer person? Is that the piloting nomenclature they taught you at…?"

Lewis interrupted by holding up the large eight-step quick-start sheet.

"Wind current is broken down in the follow-up 16-step not-as-quick instruction sheet."

"Right," I said, understanding the survival chances of this adventure were diminishing quicker than a suicidal, 4th stage pancreatic cancer patient who chose to fly United 93 on September 11, 2001.

Larry took the manila envelope given to me by the recently late Chuck Lorre. Much like my sphincter, my grip on the envelope had tightened so that my fingerprints were embedded through the envelope and on to the paper inside.

He slid a paper out from the envelope and handed to me.

CHUCK LORRE PRODUCTIONS, #288 *53

Over the years, CBS executives have always been very generous when it comes to sharing their ideas as to how I might better do my job. I have never returned the favor regarding how they might run their network. Until now. Now I have a really good idea. Step One: Create an internal division with workers who do nothing but check out the claims of prospective advertisers. And I mean really check them out. If it's a car, have somebody drive it around to see if it accelerates into walls or slow-moving pedestrians for no particular reason. If it's beer, have someone drink it and report back if it gets them laid. If it's a pill, have someone take it for a while, then wait to see if they grow a tail, get anal leakage or commit suicide. Step Two: Quality control. All commercials must be aesthetically pleasing, seriously funny, poignant or dramatic. Any commercials deemed loud, stupid and/or obnoxious are not aired. Period. No exceptions. Step Three: Tell the world that CBS only airs the coolest and most honest commercials. It's always Superbowl Sunday at CBS! Step Four: Watch the money roll in. A Final Thought: Don't worry about the initial loss of income created by dropping the dumb stuff (e.g. Cockney lizards who sell insurance). You'll more than make that money back by demanding that your high-quality advertisers cut you in for a piece of their action. You have, after all, earned it by giving them the CBS seal of approval. Another Final Thought: If you adopt my idea, my consulting fee is one million shares of CBS stock. Or better yet, one hundred shares of Apple stock.

"Hmm," I wondered out loud. It was interesting but didn't exactly give me any more answers than I already had.

"Turn it over," said Larry.

I turned it over still seeing what I had first read.

---

53 *Sometimes fiction comes very close to the reality. Sometimes, so close that you can't tell the difference between the fiction and the reality. That's one of the signs of good satire. In this case it's not close to the truth. It is the truth. This is one of the nonfictional Chuck Lorre's vanity cards. Thanks, Chuck.*

"Not all the way over," said a frustrated Larry. "Just to the back side.

"Oh."

CHUCK LORRE PRODUCTIONS, #288D [54]

…but in addition, I have to get something off my chest. For years, network executives have given me notes. They feel that their input will make my shows better. I'm not saying that the notes weren't intelligent or helpful. That's because I didn't read them. Then one day I read one of their notes. Y'know, just out of curiosity. It wasn't bad. It was horrible. I began to read the other notes. Same thing. Wretched. It was almost as if they wanted me to use the most obvious punchlines. Ones you could see coming from a mile away. The same with the concepts. Concepts that I had seen done a million times in the last thirty years. What, was I writing *Three's Company?* Network executives have no place in the writers' room. They paid me what they paid me because they knew that I knew what I was doing. Maybe I wasn't channeling Kubrick or Pinter, but I knew how to make people laugh. I thought, maybe it was a blip. They couldn't be that oblivious to what makes a show funny. So the next week, I checked the notes again. They were worse than the week before. It was almost as if they were purposely trying to make the show terrible. I thought that, compared to how they wanted me to change the show, the commercials were funnier. I'm talking about the commercials that evoked 9-11. Every week I checked and every week, same thing. Bad, bad, bad. The more I thought about it, the more I became convinced it wasn't a coincidence. The guys giving me notes weren't stupid. I'm not saying they knew how to make things funny. If they did, they wouldn't have to hire people like me overpaying to the point of embarrassment. But they must have known the notes they were giving me were deadly. Intentionally deadly. To that end, I am certain the network notes will make television unwatchable. I take that back. Unfortunately, it would be watchable, watchable enough that people who were watching it

---

54 *Now this is fiction. At least I'm pretty sure it is.*

would soon believe that what they were watching was credible. Worse… quality TV. It makes me sad. I've always been a kind of depressed person, but that has been based on uncontrollable brain chemistry reacting to the fact that I am conscious. This sadness is based on the reality of evil people doing their worst. Hugs, Chuck.

"I don't get it. Did he write two vanity cards for the same show?"

"Not exactly," said Larry. "There was one card written, but only part of what Chuck wrote was aired."

"Go on…"

"Chuck decided that he had had enough crap. He made his quadrillions doing the bidding of *the man* and he was sick and tired of his ideas having the magic taken out of them."

"So, what was with the two vanity cards?"

"Like I said, there was only one," said Larry. "The D of 288D stands for *deleted*. The stooges at the network had the second page of 288 deleted."

"Didn't Chuck stop them?"

"He tried," Lewis broke in from the front seat.

"And…?" I asked.

"Did you notice that Chuck no longer had a lower torso?" asked Larry

"To be honest… no I didn't. And really, I think it's something that I would have noticed. I mean someone floating in the air from the waist up is pretty unusual in this physical universe, except, of course, in the Arkansas suburbs. That might have made sense. But in Hollywood, I would have noticed."

Larry shook his head sadly.

"Chuck was a vain man. Having no lower torso, especially a lower torso that once contained a great exemplar of male genitals is not something you'd like to have TMZ chasing as a story. Chuck spent a great deal of his fortune working with Disney Imagineering to fashion a system of pulleys and air hooks suspending his upper torso just above his empty slacks, shoes and socks fastened below. Seriously, you would have thought there was a whole man packing those pants."

"Wait, wait, wait," I exclaimed. "What happened to his lower torso?"

"PHLEM," said Lewis, near tears.

"Chuck refused to air the show without the entire vanity card," said Larry. "Representatives from the network along with the more powerful agents from PHLEM stopped by his house to *explain* that the vanity card would be aired just as PHLEM had called for it to be. Again, Chuck, strong as he is… was… refused. The morning before the vanity card was to be aired, Chuck woke up in a bit of a haze. If you think, Jack Woltz, the film director character in *The Godfather*, was surprised by his favorite horse's head in his bed, think how Chuck felt when he tried to get out of bed to pee and found his hips and legs about a good ten feet away from his waist."

"Wow, what an amazing job. I had no idea he was anything but all Chuck."

"CGI isn't just about padding the seats in a half-filled theater when KISS performs," Richard chimed in.

"But why?" I asked.

"Did you not read the part of the vanity card that did not air?" asked Larry. "Chuck was about to tell the entire country, as well as the world five years later when that show hits syndication, that they were being scammed in the worst way."

"Holy shit."

"But there's more," warned Larry. "A lot more."

"What do you mean?"

"Do you speak French?" asked Larry.

"A little."

"How little?"

"Maybe I'm overstating my ability a wee bit. But I am familiar with most of the lyrics of 'Lady Marmalade.'"

CHAPTER THIRTY

Par le vous Burbank

BHCTF Captain O'Reilly and Detective Rich stood in front of a system of large tracking monitors intensely studying a beeping cursor heading toward "Burbank."

"He's heading toward Burbank and at the speed, height and width that can only mean he's got a UH-72A Lakota Light Utility whirlybird under him," said O'Reilly.

"Nothing we have on Young says he's capable of flying that sophisticated of a machine," said Rich.

"He's got to have some big-time shysters workin' with him, I tellya. He just ain't the type of creep who could have pulled off this big a caper alone, y'see."

"Why are you talking like some B-film gangster? asked Rich.

"I learned a long time ago that if you want to catch a bad guy, you gotta think like a bad guy."

"From the 30's?"

I ain't sayin' yes and I ain't sayin' no, but you don't catch Capone by thinking like Apatow."

"Apatow?"

"That's right. Judd Apatow."

"The comedy film director?"

"And former M.C. at the Comedy and Magic Club," exclaimed O"Reilly. "Sure, if you wanted to package Seth Rogan or Jimmy Franco in some pseudo–homosexual buddy fiasco, you go Apatow or maybe even Adam Sandler if you not concerned about it being too clever. But if you want to bring down Young or whoever the hell is behind him, you gotta go down and dirty. You go gangsta. You gotta think Suge Knight."

"You sayin' this Steve Young guy is tied up with the hip-hop underworld?"

"I don't know, but we're not going to take anything off the table."

"Nothing?"

"Nothing."

"Boots on the ground?"

"If that's what it takes," snarled O'Reilly. "But even smarter, our troops would be set up five feet off the ground so they could see above the crowds."

"We're going to have troops stand on tables?"

"Better. Hover boots."

"But…"

"Look at this," interrupted O'Reilly, pointing to the monitor.

"He's landing at Burbank Airport in, um…"

"Burbank."

"Right."

I want every car we have to head over to, um…"

"… Burbank," reminded Rich.

"Exactly."

"Got it."

Inside Larry's copter, Lewis maneuvered the helicopter down to the Burbank pad… at Burbank Airport.

"What are we doing here?" I asked.

"Why else are we at the airport. I've got my jet warming up," said Larry.

"You have your own jet?"

"I have three."

"Why three?"

"One for each season."

"But there are four seasons."

"Not since Valli went out on his own."

To almost no one's shock, other than mine, Jason Alexander peeked in through a well-placed curtain and chuckled. Then, as if there was no rationale for him to appear, he vanished as quickly as he had appeared. A diminishing chuckle faded, along with Jason.

As the chopper's propellers spun slowly to a stop, a maintenance truck sidled up to one side of the craft while a slew of some twenty 1930 Packard police cars, flashing lights spinning and sirens blaring crowded on the other side.

BHCTF officers, with rifles raised and pistols cocked, raced from their cars and up to the copter. With bullhorn in hand, Detective O'Reilly stepped from his car and up to the whirlybird (or one of the limited number of synonyms that might be substituted for helicopter).

"Alright Young. Step out with your hands up."

"Sir," said Rich, "he'd hear you better if you used the bullhorn."

"Of course," replied O'Reilly, looking at Rich with as much disdain as if he was Al Franken.

"Step out now, Young, and no one gets hurt," barked O'Reilly, through the bullhorn that rather than increase, only muffled his voice.

"The on switch is on the left side," said Rich.

With a displeased smirk O'Reilly pressed the "on" button. Rich smiled as if he had one-upped his boss. In fact, he had done just that. It was his favorite thing. And with his stanch commitment to the BHCTF there would be no time for O'Reilly to use his Factor Talking Points Memo*[55] to rip into Rich.

"Come on out, Young, and no one gets hurt," bellowed O'Reilly, through the now operational bullhorn.

Hands up, Lewis appeared at the copter's door.

"Don't shoot," yelled Lewis. "I'm allergic to bullets."

"They're gluten-free," clarified O'Reilly. "Just tell Young to come out."

"Which Young?" asked Lewis. "It's a common name."

"Steve Young," said an ever-growing, impatient O'Reilly.

"Which one? Are you not familiar with the plethora of Steve Youngs, including in the football Hall of F…"

As Lewis continued to rant, O'Reilly turned to Rich. "Get him out of there."

Officers, led by Rich, stormed the copter, snapping handcuffs on Lewis.

"It's not my copter. It's a good friend's and I don't know his name 'cause I just met him. And I left my ID with another friend who I met on the set of *COPS*," exclaimed Lewis.

"I know who you are," said Rich.

"I don't think you do. I barely know me. Haven't you seen my act?"

"Where's Young?" asked Rich.

"I don't know what you're talking about," said Lewis. "I'm the only one in here,"

"Comb through every inch of this helicopter," demanded O'Reilly.

"What?" asked Lewis.

---

55 *Bill O'Reilly would open his show with what he called a "Talking Points Memo." He used the TPM as a commentary on his view of a news item or, most often, an opportunity to demean a person or issue he disagreed with. Because he was considered a newsfotainment personality rather than a journalist he was able to say whatever he wanted without the necessity of truth coming within earshot of the TPM, which seemed to please his O'Reilly's 85-110 year old demographic.*

"The bullhorn," Rich reminded O'Reilly.

"Fuck you!" screamed O'Reilly. "I'll do it live! And without a fucking bullhorn! Comb the fucking helicopter!"

Let's be honest. How much time does it take to go through a helicopter?

"Lewis is right," said Rich. "There's no one else in here."

At the other end of the airport, a maintenance truck, the same truck that had sidled up to the helicopter, pulled up to a small jet warming its engines. The driver's side door opened and stepping from the cab was a uniformed driver with a striking resemblance to Jason Alexander. He wasn't, but when you're in the L.A. area you run into so many celebrities, especially celebrities who were bigger celebrities a few years before. The Alexander look-alike pressed the hydraulic lever and the body of the truck rose up to the jet's open hatch. Another worker, looking strikingly similar to Marie Osmond – you know, the shapely Marie who never seemed to age – glanced nervously back and forth, checking out the tarmac. Sensing she hadn't been seen, she pushed a large, draped cart from the truck into the jet.

A frustrated O'Reilly grabbed Lewis by the collar of his black collarless shirt. Unable to get a secure grip he shoved Lewis against the copter.

"Where the fuck is Young?!" O'Reilly screamed in Lewis's face, clearly unaware of appropriate proxemics, like Judge Reinhold's *close-talker* character on *Seinfeld*. Remember *Seinfeld*?

Lewis smiled as if someone had just offered him a new line of black, loose-fitting button downs.

"What's so funny?" demanded O'Reilly.

Lewis slowly turned towards a small jet, the same jet that the Marie Osmond look-alike had entered, gaining speed as it roared down a runway.

"You're fucking kidding me," O'Reilly howled.

"Vous le vous a vec moi," Lewis said with a wry smile rarely seen during his stage performance… comedy club or Carnegie (Hall and/or Deli).

"Shit," O'Reilly shouted. "He's spouting French, Frank. Get me on the next plane to Montreal."

CHAPTER THIRTY-ONE

Y'Got Company

Ztivo was in the midst of packing a small carry-on as he sat on a fun-loving twin bed in the center of a seedy motel room. Most of the seeds had yet to sprout, but due to the lack of sunlight, this was hardly a surprise.

An ominous tone, not dissimilar to the wailing of a kitty just snapped up in the jaws of a starving coyote, came from Ztivo's pocket. He had downloaded the tone from InnocentSufferingMammals.com, an app that is now an Icelandic presidential superpac. He pulled out his cell phone.

"Yes."

After a brief pause.

"I have purchased a one-way ticket…"

After a similar, but shorter brief pause.

"It will be done."

After an even briefer pause.

"Yes. Before they reach the Grail."

CUT TO:

SCENE: ABOVE THE CLOUDS A BRIGHT RED AFTERNOON SUN LIT THE SKY.

Inside a beautifully-appointed cabin, a beautifully-appointed flight attendant served a tall mimosa to Larry David.

"Thank you, Kathy."

"You're welcome, Mr. David."

The flight attendant walked to the rear compartment where she was met by a well-coifed, gray-haired, forty-something wearing surgeon scrubs. He bore a striking resemblance to Cable news anchor Anderson Cooper.

"Was that Kathy Griffin and Anderson Cooper?"

"Yes, that was Kathy. The guy who looks like Anderson Cooper is Kathy's cosmetic surgeon. She makes sure he is never more than a few feet away.

"Where exactly are we going?" I asked.

"To the one place where unsoiled television originality is stored. Hidden away from those whose only goal is to twist the writer's voice and humor from imaginative brilliance into a maniacal apparatus meant to skyrocket corporate and political profits."

"I still don't understand how…"

"In the most deceitful way known to mankind," interrupted David. "A literal and universal dumbing down of the viewer."

"I get what they're doing is morally wrong, but really, the most deceitful way known to mankind? Don't you think misleading America into a war with Iraq is a teeny bit more deceitful than serving up a punch-line that a ten-year-old in Tallahassee could see coming from a mile away?"

"Schmuck. Look at me," implored David. "Why do you think the American public bought that Iraq WMD bullshit?"

I paused for a moment. I could feel the synapses in my brain connecting Larry's words through thousands of neurons and axons; my flaccid neurotransmitters were shooting a torrid of blood through my veins into a stiff starship of brainwaves traveling at warp speed. Ah, ADD, how you amuse me.

Was he saying that dumbing down America could brainwash the public into accepting even the lowest standard of integrity as acceptable, or worse, a model of exceptionalism and honesty? Wow, clarity can generate one fucking explosion of a migraine.

"But where are we going?

"We're going where comedy is king."

"Latvia?"

Accompanied by a smirk that could have spanned the width of Levittown (Pennsylvania, not New York), Larry pulled a keyboard onto his lap. Powered on it opened a curtain in the front of the cabin exposing a large screen revealing a map of the world. With a couple of mouse clicks the screen zoomed in to a map of Paris, Texas.

"It's hidden in Texas?"

"Fuckin' auto-map-correct. Hold on a second."

A map of Paris, France appeared on the screen.

"Paris, France?" I asked. "But why?"

Larry moved his mouse over Paris and a picture of the young Jerry Lewis appeared over Paris. The sound emitted from the hit made it all clear.

"Lay-dee!"

CHAPTER THIRTY-TWO

The Flight

Uneventful.

CHAPTER THIRTY-THREE

Bienvenue a Paris

As the jet door opened, the bright lights of gay Paree shined in. It wasn't the *gay* type of Paree where you need to be fearful of people living there who are getting married to individuals who have a lot of physical similarity to each other. You know, the kind of gay that ends up sucking all the validity from your own marriage. This was Gay Paree in terms of what the word "gay" (happy, deliriously happy, happy as a lark-though there had been a lark who once took refuge in our mailbox whose *song* was quite woeful. Nothing close to happy or gay) once meant prior to it being taken hostage by those who meant to threaten our marriages by marrying each other.

"Let's go," commanded Larry. "It won't be long until PHLEM will be on to us. They've got eyes everywhere."

I didn't need a second warning. I jumped up from my seat and ran past Larry and out the jet's door.

"Wait…'" Larry warned.

Unfortunately…

"…until I drop the steps."

Luckily the distance between the jet door and the ground was slight enough, causing no broken appendages but plenty of severe pain and bruising.

Larry hurried down the stairs and dragged me into a waiting Fiat.

As we raced from the airport, I noticed that we weren't taking the same route that we would have taken based on my Mapquest directions that I had printed out in case I ever visited Paris. I always carried them with me, never knowing when the opportunity would arise. I never thought I'd have the chance unless I had garnered enough Holiday Inn points to be able to pay for the tickets. As of now, I have enough points for some chic magazines that would cost a hefty sum if not for my points.

"Larry. This isn't the way to Paris."

"We're not heading for Paris. I just wanted the police to think we were heading in that direction."

"If we're not heading for Paris, where are we going?"

Larry handed me his phone.

"We're heading to the one place that could hold the answer."

"You mean…"

"Yes," said Larry. "Damanhur."

"Exactly," I agreed with all the confidence of someone who never heard of a Damanhur.

I looked at the phone and saw our destination: Damanhur.

"What the hell is Damanhur?"

"Damanhur is a Federation of Spiritual Communities located in Italy, north of Piedmont."

I was about to use data on my cell phone to net-surf Wikipedia Damanhur info, but I was already over data quota.

"Damanhur houses the Temples of Humankind," continued Larry. "It's a huge underground facility dug entirely by hand, right into a mountain. It's full of all kinds of original art. The kind of originality that the great comedy writers have written and could continue writing if not for the powers who find so much more value in the power they strive for to fill their coffers."

"You mean that's where we find the answer to the mystery, I'm not sure I understand enough to form a lucid question with which to get an answer?"

Larry ignored me completely.

"The Temples of Humankind have been called the Eighth Wonder of the World, which I believe makes it about the 500th different Eighth Wonder of the World."

"I don't think you can legally have more than eight *Wonders*," I mused out loud. "I think it was Scalia who wrote the majority opinion. Hence the pileup at eight."

"You could be right."

A silver Fiat similar to ours pulled up close beside us. Too close. Another screeched to stop in front of our car forcing Larry to slam on the brakes. The window rolled down on the car next to the driver's side. My heart literally jumped out of my chest. Not literally. Wrong alliteration. Christ, I wish I would have sent this to an editor before getting it published.

I was expecting to see a bevy of AK-47s pointed directly at us.

Instead…

"Jimmy's here like you wanted. Jimmy needs your phone."

It was the third-person-speaking character played by *Seinfeld* actor, Anthony Starke. Amazingly, he was still using his character's name instead of his real name. It makes sense. Is there anyone who refers to the Starke episode?

Larry pulled his phone from me and handed it to Jimmy.

"Larry thanks you," said Larry.

Jimmy took off as did the car that had stopped in front of us.

"What was that about?" I asked.

Larry turned hard right and floored our car in the opposite direction that Jimmy drove.

"We're heading for The Holy Grail."

"I thought we were going to Damanhur."

"Which is exactly where O'Reilly would think we'd be going. It's known as a red herring."*[56]

Larry pulled into one of those French Sept-Onze parking lots sidling up to near the back of the building. Whizzing by, heading in the same direction as Jimmy/Anthony was another Fiat.*[57]

It carried O'Reilly and Rich.

Wow. Using the same technology (a cell phone with Maps or WAZE), that is supposed to provide seemingly great information, to give erroneous data to throw you off is about the coolest twist any author or screenwriter could use. You could almost see Tom Hanks tapping into that twist in one of his films.

Technology sucks, which begs the question: Why haven't they developed technology to unsuck itself, especially for all the pre-millennial beings who still think you're supposed to double tap the space bar after a period? It's more than just proper grammar. It's about a circadian effort to learn. That's how to become a success. It's not like the Grammar Police knocking on your door to tell you something has been changed or newly produced. Knowledge doesn't just appear within easy reach. You need to search out opportunities to learn. Remember kids, if you stop learning after your formal education ends, you'll end watching your competition bypass you in a flash. Do I really need to quote Einstein here? No. Find out yourself. Reading is fundamental.

Maybe one day there'll be technology to counter technology (the technology meant to mislead you). No doubt, it would take mere seconds

---

56 A "red herring"- not to be confused with the magenta herring Eskimos use as an erotic musk that manatee's find irresistible – is a literary device used to clarify which color herring an author or deli-man is using to confuse audiences, usually served with scrambled eggs, onion bagel and cream cheese.

57 While made in Italy I'm guessing the French dealerships do quite well and for some reason people populating the roads in this story are fans of the Italian car.

before an even newer technology would be developed to offset the new technology that had become, in mere moments, tech-nostalgia.

"Coast is clear," said Larry.

"So what now?" I asked.

"Isn't it obvious. C'est Onze de Julliet. Gratuit Sleurpea day."

Moments later, I, with a piercing Sleurpea brain-freeze headache, Larry with red syrup lips, we exited the store and climbed back into the car.

"So, where to now?"

Larry smiled and backed up the car.

"We go where we can uncover the proof of what PHLEM has wrought."

"Wrought?"

"Wrought."

How different Larry spoke off screen. Wrought? Is he planning on writing Romeo and Julio… down by the schoolyard?

The sign read "Paris 17 KM."

A second and a half later, from the other side of the Sept-Onze came a rebuilt 1954 Citroën.*58 The back of the drive's head looked familiar.

Nah. Couldn't been.

Moments later we were speeding along a narrow, winding, mountain highway, our Fiat zigzagging in and around magnificent views suited perfectly for a Kia Soul television commercial labeled with a strong warning this was to be done only if you're a professional driver on a closed course.

With the gas pedal pressed tightly to the floor, every turn challenged the tires keeping us from spinning airborne. There was no doubt that Larry knew where he was going and getting there as quickly as humanly/

58 Thereyago, just a page before noting that there was nothing but Fiats coating the French countryside, a Citroën pops up. It's not so much the Citroën reveals that there are cars besides Fiats. Fact is, they're produced in France, but that I had never seen a Citroën before. That it surfaces during this story, one I'm writing, well, that's just the magic of literature.

automobily possible was the only thing on his mind. Obviously, that was an assumption on my part as Larry refused to tell me what or how many things were on his mind.

I glanced at the rear-view mirror to see the Citroën fast approaching. Too fast. Dangerously fast.

"Larry," I cautioned. "There's some guy behind us who's getting really close."

Larry took a peek at the mirror. For the first time in our adventure, I saw fear in his eye. Not both. Just the left eye. The one closest to me. His right eye was fearless.

"Shit! It's Ztivo."

"Michael Ztivo?" I asked.

"No Mahatma Ghandi Ztivo. Of course, Michael Ztivo."

Mahatma Ghandi Ztivo was a second cousin Michael used to make his Bollywood deals.

"I don't understand."

Ignoring me, Larry focused on his driving, seeming to push his foot through the floor. Barely hugging the road, every turn a test of gravity… a multiple-choice test. Could have been true of false. Most importantly, failure was unacceptable.

Bam!

"Fuck!" Larry exclaimed.

Obviously, a Citroën is faster than a Fiat… probably even faster than a Kia Soul. We were rear-ended in a far more powerful and intimate manner than my wife would have ever allowed me to if she had been in the Fiat's place.

Larry struggled to keep our car on the road. To say I was scared would be an understatement. "VERY scared" would be less ambiguous.

"What's this all about?!" I asked screamingly, for perhaps the twentieth time in the past two days.

Again, Larry was far more intent on keeping our car from skidding off the side of the road. Did I happen to mention that when I say side of the road, there was no side of the road? It was just a long drop off into a ravine thousands of feet below.

I looked back to see the Citroën once again approaching ever closer, close enough to see the driver's face. It was Michael Ztivo, the Hollywood super-agent who once ruled the industry like Vlad III, Prince of Wallachia.*[59]

Before I could make one more evil reference, Ztivo slammed into our Fiat sending us flying off the road.

I didn't remember what happened next if, in fact, anything did.

---

59 Vlad III (also known as Vlad the Impaler) who was many times confused with Vlad IV (also known as Vlad the Impala for his penchant for his collection of African Antelopes). In the mid-1400s III executed his enemies by vicious impalement. He was a fan of various forms of torture including disemboweling and rectal and facial impalement. Surprisingly, this was the least of his negatives. A poll taken in 1458 showed III's executions with a 57% favorable rating. His polls dropped radically when he refused to take his ninety-year-old mother to dinner on her birthday.

CHAPTER THIRTY-FOUR

It Was an Exceptionally Uneventful Life

I struggled to open my eyes. They were stuck closed as if I was awakening out of a long coma. That could be the good news. If I was coming out of a coma that meant I lived through whatever happened. I mean I remember being slammed into by the Citroën, but that was all I remember.

I continued to struggle with my eye lids attempting to pull themselves apart. I could almost hear the lids slowly separating, creating the slightest slit through which I was blasted by a piercing, bright light. Made sense. I had no idea how long my eyes were closed, but even waking from an overnight sleep you need some time to adjust.

As my eyes began to adapt to the light, I was surprised at what I saw: light. Nothing but light. White light. Nothing else. I blinked a few times attempting to focus on something. Anything. Still, all I saw was a stark, bright void. I looked around. To my right. To my left. Up, down and behind. Just to make sure my eyes weren't playing a trick on me, I checked again, but this time I reversed the strategy. Behind, down and up. To my left. To my right. Same result. Nothing.

Oh, my God. Am… am… am I dead?

"Steve."

What?!

"Over here."

I thought I had checked everywhere, but for some reason, I had never checked northwest. Floating down from above-northwest above was a snowy-bearded figure sporting a long, white robe. He stopped about three feet from the ground. Softly in the background, an angelic voice sang what I first thought was "The Battle Hymn of the Republic." Wait a minute. It wasn't that Glory, Glory Hallelujah thing. It was "Hello," and the voice was Adele's. So odd since Adele's voice was not even on the horizon and "Hello" had yet to be written. Crazy.

"A little help."

Holy crap. God was asking me – me, little insignificant me – for help.

"What makes you think I'm God." said the vision I had thought was God.

"But I didn't say that out loud," I said.

"You think that every schmuck who mind-reads is God?"

"So, you're not God?"

"I didn't say that."

"Then you are?"

"I didn't say that either. Your judgements seem to bend with the slightest breeze. Have you no real conviction?"

"Sorry, I haven't been dead before."

"Could you please… help me down."

"Huh?"

"I need a bit of a tug."

"God needs…"

"I am not God."

I walked over to the fella who was suspended several feet off the ground.

"What do you need me to do?

"Just pull."

I grabbed around the knees and pulled.

"That's enough," he said.

I let go and he floated to the ground.

"We're still trying to get the kinks out of the pulley system."

"What the hell is happening?" I asked.

"Perhaps you should be asking, 'what is NOT happening.'"

As he said that he pulled off his beard and long white robe, and left standing before me was Dick Van Dyke, a very young Dick Van Dyke. *Dick Van Dyke Show* young. *Bye Bye Birdie* young.

"Mr. Dyke," I said, reverently.

"The name is Petrie. Rob Petrie."

"I get it. The character you played on *The Dick Van Dyke Show*."*[60]

"No, I am Rob Petrie. The head writer on the *Alan Brady Show*."

"Okay. I'm not sure what you're up to but…"

"Hiya doin', Steve."

Walking up and stopping next to Dick, or Rob, was Phil Silvers.

"Mr. Silvers…"

"Bilko's the name. Sargent Ernie Bilko."

"From *You'll Never Get Rich*."

"Some know it as *Sergeant Bilko*," I replied, proud of trivial 50's TV knowledge.

"Hey d'ere."

"Carroll O'Conner, from *All in the Family*."

"Bunker's the name. Archie Bunker."

---

60 *I can't believe I have to write this but I was hoping someone under fifty would be reading, so here goes: The Dick Van Dyke Show was created by Carl Reiner where actor Dick Van Dyke played Rob Petrie, the head writer of the Alan Brady variety show. Carl Reiner played Alan Brady.*

THE LARRY DAVID CODE

"O-o-oh. Nevermind," said, Gilda, er, um, Rosanne Rosannadanna.

And like the comedy gods opened the gates of originality, people, um, characters, seem to appear out of nowhere.

Hawkeye Pierce (Alan Alda), Barney Fife (Don Knotts), Ralph Kramden and Ed Norton *[61] (Jackie Gleason and Art Carney), Kingfish (Tim Moore), Ted Baxter (Ted Knight), Joan Stevens (Joan Davis), Larry Sanders (Gary Shandling) and a load more.

"I don't get it."

"And you wouldn't," said Petrie, "if it weren't for the great comedy writers who created us."

"Okay. I get that, but what does this have to do with me? What's all this supposed to mean? Am I going through some end-of-life revelation? Am I dead and this is heaven? I mean I appreciate the entertainment value here, but if this is it, with this as my eternal resting place, I would hope that's there's more than old television characters. I would far more appreciate great amounts of luscious food with no weight gain, Mark Zuckerberg wealth, and of course, sex with no guilt."

"Your depth of value impresses me," said Petrie. "You hoped to one day enter the gates of comedy sovereignty with its bountiful rewards, yet you ignore the significance of television's literary giants. Those were the ones who opened the door for me and these other great characters – the ones like Norman Lear who made racism and bigotry hysterical, yet teaching opportunities, the ones like Alan Zweibel who made *Saturday Night Live* unmissable (partially by co-creating the character Roseanne Roseannadanna with Gilda Radner) and *It's Garry Shandling's Show,* a breakthrough in design and satire, a template for breaking the fourth wall, ones like Bernie Fein and Al Ruddy who made Nazi concentration camps

---

61 *This is not Ed Norton, the fine, anorexic actor who could only confuse the issue more if he were cast to portray character Ed Norton in a Honeymooners film remake of the classic Honeymooners. As we all know the film would become in instant film classic as all other remakes such as "Sergeant Bilko," "Get Smart," "Bewitched," "McHales Navy" and "60 Minutes."*

a punchline in *Hogan's Heroes* and the ones like Carl Reiner who made *The Dick Van Dyke Show's* Laura Petrie both funny, adorable and overwhelmingly fuckable."

"No, no. You have it all wrong. I worship the writers, the characters they created and their classic shows."

"Ahem…" interrupted Ed Norton, who then waved his hands in preparation for the prerequisite ten seconds before Ralph Kramden slammed him on the shoulder with his hat.

"Will you…!!!" yelled Kramden.

"Then why aren't you doing everything you can to keep producing, um, what you call, invocation?" asked Norton.

"Innovation, idiot," corrected Kramden.

"I am doing everything," I said.

"No, Vegetable-head," said O'Conner. "You're just running away."

"Maybe, at first," I said. "But now I'm wanted for a murder I'm not sure actually happened. I've flown from the United States to Paris while the police are trying to arrest me for more murders. I've got some maniacal nutcase, who used to be the most powerful man in Hollywood, trying to track me down and kill me. And right now, it seems like he might have succeeded."

"The point is you've got to find out who's trying to kill TV," said Hawkeye.

"Exactly," I said. "And that's why I'm going wherever Larry takes me."

"Well, my friend. Larry isn't taking you anyplace." A familiar voice emerged from behind me.

"What?"

"Anymore."

Through a cloud of white, dramatically walked Larry David.

"I'm no longer there to help you."

"Huh?"

"Because, Steve… I'm dead. As dead as Scott Baio's career."

"I don't understand."

"The crash. It was fatal."

"Fatal?"

"As fatal as a network vice president of development's gag pitch. You're on your own kid."

"You mean I'm supposed to save TV comedy by myself?"

"You really don't get it, do you?" said Larry who appeared from a cloud of smoke wafting from O'Conner's cigar. "This isn't about saving comedy. This is about saving humanity."

A resounding round of laughter filled the air.

"What the hell?!"

"We are here with everyone who played a part in our business," said Petrie.

Convulsing laughter.

"That's Charley Douglass," whined Barney Fife. "He's the sound engineer who created the laugh track."

Shocked oohs and ahhs melded into annoying giggling.

"Charlie!!!" screamed Kramden.

"Yep. There were a lot of shows that needed to alert audiences that what was said or happened was funny," explained Petrie.

"Tee-hee."

"CHAR-LIE!" all chimed in.

"Laugh tracks or what I like to call, canned laughter, do have a place," said Ted Baxter. "Not for me. I didn't need any help. Neither did my anchor doppelgänger, Walter Cronkite. Now Mary, she could use all the help she could get. I wouldn't say she was soft. More malleable."

"Larry, if you're dead, aren't I also dead," I asked. "I mean we were both in the same car."

"Steve, why is it that you seem to think what happens to me should happen to you? I'm me. You're you. We both might be writers, but there is a difference."

"Font choice?" I guessed.

"Talent." Larry quickly corrected. "As well as success, which is hardly under your control. There's no guarantee. Unless you're God or Spielberg. Wait… He did produce *The Flintstones* film, so… yeah… Success is not under your control. But talent… There is a clear difference between us."

"Wow. That clears it up for me. Thanks for seriously feeding my lack of self-esteem. I was afraid that it was diminishing at too slow a rate."

"Hey, schmuck. I just said that you hold in your hands the survival of humanity. If you accomplish that and it doesn't produce some sense of competence in you, God help us all."

"Can you give me something I can hang my hat on? To show people. Something that proves there's some tangible evidence proving there's a clear effort to tear down America and society?"

"You want something? You want something that puts the nail in the coffin?"

"It would help."

"Okay. How's this? You ever watch *Seinfeld*?

I smirked, rolled my eyes and added a couple other dismissive moves that illustrated the many nonverbal examples of indifferent communication.

"Do you really think I wanted to use Kathy Griffin in the show? And more than once? I was forced to in an attempt to bring in the 'not that there's anything wrong with it,' the 'other team' so-to-speak audience. I loaded up Jerry with the most beautiful women in the world, most of whom wouldn't have given him a second look if it weren't for the fact I casted them in those roles. Then… BAM. The network note came down demanding I book Griffin."

"I kind of think Griffin is hot."

"Don't get me wrong. I would have done Kathy before the surgeries. Then again, I would have done Anderson Cooper. *Seinfeld* were my horniest years."

"So, you're saying that when society asks why they should believe there is an evil and powerful consortium that has been dumbing down America to sell poor products and elect corrupt leaders who are not working in the best interests of the people, I should point to the network having you book Kathy Griffin."

"I admit, not the best example, but I've taken you as far as I can take you. I gave you something you can wrap your head around. I didn't tell you that it was the most effective example. You're going to have to find the Holy Grail on your own. Once you have it, put that into words and tell the world."

I was stunned. Stunned that he believed that I could handle something so big, so important.

"Or you can walk away and choose to spend your life writing for OAN."

"Are they hiring?"

Larry shot me his finest scrutinizing squint, very similar to the nonfiction Larry David (when he plays the fictional Larry David in *Curb Your Enthusiasm*) squint. He was right, I had made it all about me. I had to let him know I was taking this seriously.

"I was kidding."

Another squint.

"So, the answer is in me," I declared.

"Brilliant. But first you need to find the cryptex. You find the cryptex, you'll find the answer."

"Okay. Okay. Find the cryptex. I get it."

"Right. Good. Then my job here is finished."

His voice began to fade…

"My job here is finished…"

As did his image.

"My job here is finished."

"Wait, I have a question!"

"For crissakes," said a clearly agitated Larry. "What is it?"

"Um. What is a cryptex?"

"Are you serious?" asked Larry, impatiently.

"What?"

"I said, 'Are you serious?!'"

"Yes, I'm serious. Maybe some people know what a cryptex is, but I never heard of it and if I never heard of it how am I supposed to find it? To tell you the truth I don't even know how to spell it, let alone what it means. Is it cri- or cry-? Is there any letter between r and p?"

"You'll know everything when you're supposed to. Trust me."

"I'm serious here. If this is heaven, or some sort of an afterlife, is there a God? Is God there?"

"That you cannot know until you are officially dead," said Larry.

"Wait, wait, wait. I can barely hear you."

"Shit. How's this?"

"Much better."

"You can't get the facts about what happens after you die, until you are officially dead," said Larry, much louder.

"Okay. Not understanding at all."

Larry took an exasperated breath. Then gave it right back.

"It doesn't happen just because you stop breathing for ten, twenty minutes. Y'gotta be dead for at least a week. They changed the rules during the near-death experience boom of '04. A ton of people were saying they had died and went to heaven where they would meet someone, they knew who had died. Somehow the dead people they met who were ill when alive were not only now healthy, but they were younger than when they died. Medical advancements in heaven are stunningly effective. Still, these healthy, except for being deceased, individuals were spreading ridiculous stories that could never happen. Or they would say they met Christ or Moses or Apollo Creed. Then they'd describe what heaven looked like and from what I've heard from sincerely dead people, it looks nothing like that. They made it sound so good, there was a significant increase in people committing suicide, not because life was terribly hopeless for them, but because they had heard that heaven was so fuckin' great. And that's total bullshit. I mean, heaven might be pretty good, but not as good these so-called dead people described it."

"What is the heaven really like?" I asked.

"Well, for one thing, you're able to see through clothing and…"

He stopped DEAD in his tracks, giving me that adorable Larry smile.

"I'm not really sure yet. I need another six or seven days dead before it's clear to me."

"So, if a person is only dead for minutes or hours that person is not counted as really dead yet," I said. "Like you."

"I didn't say I wasn't dead. Can't you see through me and my clothes?"

"Could I try that out on Laura Petrie?"

"You're a perv."

"You're a perv."

"You're a perv"

Larry's voice echoed softer and softer.

The scene itself, dimmer and dimmer.

I felt like I was being sucked into a well-lit dark hole. Not so much pitch black. It was a layered darkness. More like ten or twenty shades of grey (or gray). Still, the figures and sounds of moments ago had faded away.

Was I heading away from death… or into it? It's one of those great questions that you rarely have the opportunity to ask. That's why, when the opportunity arose, I took it. As Einstein said, and I will incessantly repeat: within every difficulty lies opportunity.

Einstein. Me. Two peas in a pod.

How thrilled he would be.

CHAPTER THIRTY-FIVE

Resurrection

Ztivo stood on the narrow road overlooking the smoking Fiat hundreds of feet below. If you looked closely, very closely, you could almost see a smile. Not a normal person smile. Think of how Hitler might have smiled when he played with his dogs in those black and white 8mm films. Or when he watched Aryan children frolic. Or when he executed a Jew.

He answered his cell phone as its ringtone played "Copacabana." Not the Barry Manilow version. Adam Lambert's.

"It is done."

(Beat)

"Very done."

(Beat)

"Well done. Seared to a crisp. Like perfect French fries. Unrecognizable as fries, but still, tasty."

For the most part, getting a restaurant to make your fries that crispy is at best a long shot. The waiter assures you he knows what you mean, but back in the kitchen, they think they understand better than you. If I'm at Ruth Chris, maybe. But I'm talking about a diner. A fuckin' diner. Just make it the way I told you to make it.

Ztivo snapped his phone closed, stuffed it in his pocket and gave a knowing wink. Then, almost immediately, after rubbing his eye, he pulled a tiny gnat from it. Comparatively, the difference between a tiny gnat and a large gnat doesn't mean as much to most people unfamiliar with the culex pipiens family of flying insects. But to another gnat, this gnat would be considered a dwarf.

Nevertheless, it hadn't been a knowing wink at all. It was a gnat that flew into his eye.

A teaching moment: never assume anything.

Ztivo walked to his car, a Peugeot. A fuckin' Peugeot. It wasn't a Citroën at all. How in the world could I have made that mistake? I mean, sure, it's an Italian-manufactured car but really, they don't look all that much alike. If we are to learn anything from this story, don't depend on me when selecting your next car.

Ztivo climbed into his car and with one more glance back at his triumph, he wheeled out.

CHAPTER THIRTY-SIX

Crash Aftermath: The Movie

Act III Scene 3

As Ztivo DRIVES off we PAN over the road and down the hill to where the SMOLDERING car SMOLDERS. We CLOSEUP on Larry David. He is MOTIONLESS, his bloody head PRESSED deeply into the driver's air bag. We CIRCLE his body SETTLING UPON a TEAR RUNNING DOWN his face representing all the repressed sadness he has stifled that only death could release, and in so, letting go of the pain. In a way, this is a good thing. (The release of every other body fluid is something you can read about in my New Yorker article for *While Death is Sad it is Far More Disgusting.*") The passenger seat where Steve Young was seated prior to the plunge off the road is CRUSHED but Young is nowhere in the car. We PAN the CRASH scene SURVEYING the hillside. A BODY lay against a large rock near the top of the hill. CLOSINGUP on the still body it is difficult to tell whose body it is though you can see from the back that he is wearing the same clothes Young was wearing in the previous scene in the Fiat. Could he be dead? We're in the middle of the second act, start of the third at best. Really. There have been no other major characters introduced substantial enough who would be able to replace Young as the protagonist, so you can pretty much expect that in the next few seconds… LOOK! He's beginning to stir. Slowly at first. He's in pain but most of his wounds seem to be superficial. He TURNS to the CAMERA and though covered with dirt and feces left there from a nearby suburban French mountain goat herd, there's no doubt that this is Young.

And SCENE.

Was I alive?

"Ow."

Can you feel pain in heaven?

"Ow."

Wait. I think that feeling pain thing is about whether you're dreaming or not.

"Ouch."

Okay, I wasn't dreaming. The question is whether I wasn't dreaming while alive or I wasn't dreaming while I was dead.

For the record, I didn't know. But being that there is no record (or as you kids refer to: a cassette tape) for this book, certainly no permanent record, I was going to go with alive. If I was wrong… if I was wrong, my problems were far worse than whether there's a "y" in cryptex. 'Cause there is.

I didn't know the French law, but I guess not securing my seat belt and getting thrown out of the car was a solid involuntary move. I had seen enough movies to know that only the living can feel pain. I just hoped I wasn't so alive that I would be in unbearable pain. I felt around my face. Seemed like everything was still there. I rubbed my arms, my torso, my legs. Much to my amazement, the pain wasn't all that severe. Uncomfortable. Yes. Sore like a bruise. Didn't seem to be any broken bones. A cat scan days later would prove that I did have a slight concussion. (Reminder: Call Mel, my attorney) Finally. All my friends who played contact sports had suffered through concussions. Me? Nevah! I was more a noncontact sport advocate… debate, chess, pep club, never participating, but enthusiastically advocating for others being allowed to participate. I had once broken a finger applauding far too, um, enthusiastically, a mathlete competition. An overreaction on my part. The competitor from my school has gotten the answer wrong. Who knew? Still, with this concussion I could say that I too knew what it was like to concuss through actual physical contact. That day I had become a man… and yet, not a single bar mitzvah gift.

I pulled myself up. I felt like I had been in a non-sanctioned UFC match with a fighter who could beat me easily but was gentlemanly enough to leave me semi-conscious.

Surveying the scene, my eyes caught sight of the Fiat below, still smoldering. Panic began to set in. I stood up and ran/limped noticeably towards the crash site. With all the difficulties I had been through, it was always about me, me, me. But now it was about someone else. Did Larry survive? Or was my hallucination of heaven or limbo, not a hallucination at all.

The heat from the flames made it difficult to get close enough to pull Larry from the car. His face was ashen, not so much an ashen color but more because most of his body had turned to ash.

My guess was that he was gone.

I hoped that he hadn't suffered. Then again, even surviving a severe car crash with the accompanying injuries, then slowly burning, feeling the torment of your skin boiling down to your bone before you pass out, it's got to be a bit uncomfortable. Then, what if just before your heart stops beating due to asphyxiation, for just a moment, a single moment, you regain consciousness to feel what would have to be unimaginable agony. You can clearly understand that it's got to be incredibly painful.

Though I felt lost at that moment, I had been lost many times before. Just catch me in the middle of trudging through constructing a decent second act. But I had never sensed a loss of such magnitude as at that moment. Larry had believed in me and given me a powerful sense of being, a meaning for my life. Why had he selected me above everyone else to carry out such an important and monumental task? Sometimes… many times, a person needs another to believe in him before he can believe in himself. And I can say with the utmost confidence, a few had less belief in themselves than I had in myself.

I thought the proper thing to do was to wait for the car to cool off and pull out (what was left of) Larry and give him a proper burial. But by that time, all that would be left of him would be ashes. Certainly cremation was a burial option. In this case, there were no other option. I stood as close to the car as I could and looked for the words that would suffice.

You know how they say you should quiet yourself, allowing you to hear that part of you where the truth lives. When you do that, you'll know what to say.

So that's what I did.

After about five or six minutes of silence, I didn't hear anything but the breeze. A very sharp and noisy breeze. A breeze so strong that it pretty much blew whatever was left of Larry swirling into the air. There was something very spiritual about the moment. Larry had made close to a billion dollars from Seinfeld alone. Here he was, dead to the world, and yet a billion specks floated joyfully, almost alive, through the air, at one point linking together forming the word "SATIRE." To be perfectly honest, it looked more like "$ATIre." Sloppy to be sure but getting the case and fonts to line up perfectly when you're speaking of the serendipity of float-ing ashes, that's close enough. I mean it's not near as clear as a *Forest Gump* floating feather, but what is?

"Ironic," I said softly.

I don't think I could have expressed what Larry meant to the world more perfectly. He reversed the comedy landscape. Those in power had meant to restrict creativity by promoting boiler plate programs as the stan-dard for quality television. They put on bad television and called it *innova-tive* programming.

It's such a scam. If you write cleverly, it's considered elitist. If it's substantial, it's said to be "about nothing." Consequently, they get to produce substandard products and the public thinks them to be quality merchandise.

Wait, maybe "ironic" is the wrong word. Paradoxical? Dry? Sardonic? Nah, it's ironic.

It was almost at that moment that an ash flew into my eye. My immediate reaction was to rub out the ash. I touched my eyeball softly lifting the speck onto the tip of my finger. About to flick it off, something stopped me. I looked, excuse me, *eye-balled* the ash and saw, not a speck of ash but something deeper. A speck of Larry. I had Larry David on the tip of my finger. It could have felt like the most powerful moment of my creative life. This was more than some abstract thought. This was literally a physical part of Larry. Granted it was about the tiniest particle of a person one could imagine. Got to be honest. The speck probably didn't have any of Larry's DNA on it. Deoxyribonucleic acid degrades at about 700°. But maybe the car fire never reached 700° so that it remained an actual physical portion of Larry.

I wondered for a fraction of a moment if the ash might be cloneable, that another Larry could carry on his greatness. The fact that I had absolutely no idea how to clone a person or any other organic item, squashed those thoughts.

This would be the last time I could be this close to Larry.

I attempted to press Larry's ash against my cornea, but my eye has always been very sensitive to touch. Kept me from using contact lenses. I needed an alternative entry. That's when I realized that I had a ton of choices on my face alone. It didn't take long before I chose.

I went nasal. I had never gone nasal before but when you truly care about someone, what might seem abnormal or perverse to some people, to another it's just eccentric. I pushed Larry's ash as deep as I could into my left nostril. The penetration was tight at first but after relaxing a bit, the ash slid smoothly, gently into my nasal passage. It felt right. Like more than a one-time thing. Larry had entered me and we were one.

CHAPTER THIRTY-SEVEN

Damanhur

Blinking lights spinning and Frank Rich blowing a loud whistle out the passenger window, O'Reilly's Fiat pulled Jimmy's Fiat over to the side of the road, stopping next to a road sign reading "Damanhur 1.27359 KM."*[62] With nine millimeter handguns pulled, O'Reilly and Rich warily approached Jimmy's car.

"Stick your hands out the window," shouted O'Reilly.

"Jimmy's gonna put his hands out the window," replied Jimmy.

"Not fucking Jimmy," yelled O'Reilly. "You, driver. Put your hands out the window."

"Jimmy's doing exactly what you want."

Jimmy stuck both hands out the window.

"The guy's stoned," Rich whispered to O'Reilly.

"Step out of the damn car," shouted Rich.

"Jimmy's getting out of the car," said Jimmy.

"Driver," yelled O'Reilly. "Out of the car, now!"

Jimmy stepped out of the car.

"Hands up and walk back to me," demanded Rich.

Jimmy walked back.

---

62 *Due to the confusion created by Damanhur being located on the border of Damanhim road signs in the area needed to be very specific.*

"Jimmy's doing what you said to do," said Jimmy.

"Who the hell is Jimmy?" asked O'Reilly.

Ready to explain, Jimmy turned toward O'Reilly.

"Jimmy is…"

Bam!

With a shot delivered perfectly between his eyes, Jimmy collapsed to the ground.

"Jimmy's dead," Jimmy might have thought.

O'Reilly stood there with a smoking pistol.

"Bill. You shot the fuckin' guy."

"I thought he was he was reaching for an AK-47," said a shaken O'Reilly.

"His hands were up," said Rich.

"Only two of them."

"What the fuck are you talking about? You shot an unarmed man."

"Ah, that's just more of your liberal Alinsky Chomsky mumbo jumbo. Do you realize what he was capable of?"

"You really aren't serious, are you?"

O'Reilly, pistol cocked, rushed towards Jimmy's car.

"Enough of your crap," O'Reilly said. "Where's Young and David?"

Rich followed O'Reilly to the car and rummaged through it.

"No sign of Young or David," said Rich.

O'Reilly pulled out a cell phone from under the front seat.

"Fuck," exclaimed O'Reilly. "We were duped. This is David's phone. He could be miles from here now."

O'Reilly rushed back to the car with Rich at his heels.

"What about this guy?" asked Rich. "We can't just leave him for the vultures."

O'Reilly opened his car door.

"Hey, the guy was asking for it."

"What the hell are you talking about? You shot him for no reason!"

"No, I didn't."

"Yes, you did."

"I just guess we'll have to agree to disagree."

"Nothing you say is making sense."

"Agreed."

Rich shook his head and got into the car as O'Reilly wheeled out, spinning back from whence he came.

CHAPTER THIRTY-EIGHT

Chuck DeGaulle Airport Terminal… Very Terminal

A jet-black jumbo jet rolled up to a Terminal 12½A. The aircraft had no identification except for a tiny "Honk if You're Horny" bumper sticker on the rear flap of the right wing.

On the ground were at least twenty black-uniformed, hooded guards, all armed with large, powerful weapons. The heftiest of the soldiers carried weapons that looked more bazooka than rifle. As with the jet, there were no identification markers on the uniforms of the guards, except for one "Don't blame me, I voted for Nader… Oops, NVM" sticker on the back of one helmet.

Instead of a ramp or a walkway being run out to the aircraft, a double-decker bus, windows blackened, drove out and was raised on hydraulics to the jet doorway.

Once the passengers emptied out of the jet the bus began to lower, revealing two flight attendants waving their goodbyes from the plane's door. A single window on the bus rolled down as a thick rifle barrel extended out aimed directly at the waving flight crew. Two successive blasts thundered from the rifle nailing each flight attendant in the heart, driving them back into the jet leaving a bloody pile of formerly pleasant, flight-worthy, "coffee-or-soda?" serving lives stacked neatly against the wall of the flight deck.

As the window rolled up the bus drove away. The guards stepped onto another waiting black bus which followed the first bus across the tarmac and out the gates onto the highway.

Note: My memory isn't what it once was, but I believe there was some pretty ominous music playing the bus off the tarmac.

CHAPTER THIRTY-NINE

We'll Always Have Paree

I made my way up to one of those countryside cottages that seemed to be the focus of every French postcard I'd ever seen. Obviously, I was discounting the black and white French postcards I would regularly find in my grandfather's nightstand. Most of the men and women in my grandfather's day wore rectangular black masks over their eyes in their postcards so I couldn't be sure if the people in those cards were French as much as naked.

I crept up to a small Tesla three-seater sitting in front of the cottage. The owners were obviously ahead of their time. I opened the door slowly and reached under the dashboard seeking the wires that I could use to start the car. Unfortunately, when I see actors do this in such an easy manner in the movies, never revealing their hands, I had no idea what you had to do get the car started. Luckily, and in a most contrived story-twist even a sightless toddler could imagine, an ignition key was lying on the floor.

If only it was the ignition key to this car.

Well, it wasn't.

But luckily, right next to that ignition key was another key and that key slid into the ignition as a smoothly as horny fifteen-year-old boy would slide his penis into an overripe mango. *63

I started the car and drove off.

63 *Just like integrity in a political campaign, I'm running out of metaphors.*

In the rear-view mirror, I saw the family who lived in the cottage run out of the house. Oddly, they appeared to be upset, their mouths miming rage, yet I could not hear a word. It's so amazing to what extent a missing muffler and closed windows can distort sound.

I hit the road, still not sure where I was going other than knowing that I had to get away.

After driving a few kilometers, I noticed, in the distance, a similar car that I had last seen O'Reilly in. By the size of the head in the driver's seat and the tsunami of bullshit flowing from it, it had to be O'Reilly. He must have noticed me in his mirror as he swerved across the road to block my way. I took a quick right (it could have been a left, but not as quick) off onto a dirt road. I floored it and soon came upon a small church-like building that had a sign on it.

"L'église"

Wished my French was better. Wished it existed at all. For all I knew it could have been a synagogue or a marijuana silo or even a Scientology bookstore where I once saw Tom Cruise shopping. It really didn't matter all that much what kind of building it was. All that mattered was that it could be a place where I could hide from O'Reilly.

I parked my car around the back of the building. I found an unlocked door and completely unnoticed by anyone, slipped in, hoping that if anyone was in there, they wouldn't see that I…

"Bonjour."

Out of nowhere appeared a hulk of a man dressing in a dirty white t-shirt and dirtier overalls. His toothless smile was disarming. To be perfectly honest, he wasn't completely toothless. There was a fragment of a molar still hanging in there.

He grabbed my hand with a firm grip, shaking it like he was about to interview for a job.

"Bonjour," I said, exhausting most of my French vocabulary.

"Première fois ici?"

I figured the jig, French vocab-wise, was up.

"I don't speak French."

"Oh, you're American?"

"You speak English?"

"Just the phrase 'Oh, you're American.'"

"But…"

"It's not important. You're in the right place. We're about to start."

Waving me on, he walked down a flight of stairs. I followed him down and through double doors into a large room where about fifteen people sat on folding chairs in a circle. He urged me to follow him as he walked to the front of the room and sat at a small table facing the group. He directed me to sit at the chair next to him. He picked up a small wooden gavel and rapped it twice on the table.

"Je m'appelle Peter, un alcoolique."

"Bonjour, Peter," responded the group.

I don't speak French, but I didn't have to be Charles Aznavour to know that this was an Alcoholics Anonymous meeting.

"Since our guest here is an American and we all are able to speak English…"

"What about me?" ask one livid, elderly chap. "I don't speak English."

"Gerard," said Peter. "You taught me English."

"Ah-h-h." growled Gerard. "You make me sick."

"Our American friend… I'm sorry, since it is your first time here, could you please tell us your name?"

"Thank you," I said. "I'm Steven, and I am an alcoholic."

I was never sure if I was a true alcoholic. I never lived in a cardboard box. I mean I slept in a box, but the box was in the middle of my Valley apartment. But seriously, there was no better place in L.A. to network than A.A. Then again, I did drink about seven or eight Southern Comfort Manhattans, the hundred proof stuff, a day, so…

"Bonjour, Steven," droned the group.

At the back of the room, through the same door, came O'Reilly.

"Young!" roared O'Reilly.

Like a wounded rhino who just spotted his lover being sodomized by a notorious horny hippo who was known to slip unnoticed into the herd by strapping on an empty water-ice cone to his forehead, O'Reilly charged through the room making a beeline for me. Like most angry rhinos, O'Reilly wasn't all that careful, knocking attendees off their chairs.

"You're done, Young," snarled O'Reilly as he grabbed my collar and hoisted me into the air.

Before I could even think the word, "shit," Peter and Gerard pulled O'Reilly off me and held him down as the rest of the group pummeled the so-called sexual predator and bogus historian.

"No one invades this sacred space and dares attack any of our brothers," said Peter with great Anger. Anger Girard was big.

Not one to ignore an escape opportunity, I pulled away from the brawl and snuck out the same door I came in.

"Don't you know who I am?!" cried out O'Reilly.

"No, we don't." declared Peter.

"I'm Bill O'Reilly."

"From Fox News?" asked Gerard in English.

"Formerly," said O'Reilly, sheepishly.

The pummeling intensified.

CHAPTER FORTY

On The Way Out from Whence I Came

Outside the l'église, I was about to climb back into my car when I felt what seemed like the barrel of a large pistol trying to inject itself deep into my kidneys.

"Turn around, slowly," said a familiar, though not all that familiar, voice.

I did so and found myself staring into the eyes of Frank Rich, O'Reilly's second in command.

"Going somewhere, Mr. Young," said Rich with a hint of a smile.

"Humina, humina."

I really had no idea why I threw out a Ralph Kramden nervous tick. It was more of a cartoonish stall than it was an act of defiance.

"What do you guys want from me?" The words were barely able to slide out of my mouth.

"To tell you the truth, while it is my job to apprehend and bring to justice any and all who strive to diminish the sacrosanct Hollywood society, really, I could give a good flying fuck."

"Huh?"

"Young. I don't know whether you are responsible for these crimes, but my guess is, if O'Reilly thinks you're guilty, there's a better than even chance you're not."

"Wow. Thanks."

"No need to thank me. It has nothing to do with you. It's just about how much I hate O'Reilly."

"Does that mean you're going to let me go?"

"Not exactly."

At that exact moment he smacked me across my forehead with the handle of his gun. I did my best nosedive, similar to a deflated, unwanted sex doll collapsing to the ground moaning like a fatally wounded antelope. It was my standard go-to whenever I was attacked anywhere from my groin up. I grabbed my head, then looked at my hands that were overflowing with globs of thick red blood. My thick red blood.

"I thought you didn't think I was guilty," I said from my fetal position as I laid on the rocky countryside. "Why'd you smack me with your gun?"

It was only then that I realized that I not only had a deep gash in my head but I had fallen head first into a pile of goat shit. French goat shit. The finest goat shit in the world.

"Shit," I exclaimed. "What is your story?"

"Don't be an idiot," Rich said. "Get up."

Dizzy and quite nauseous, I struggled to my feet.

"Schmuck," said Rich. "I had to make it look like I put up a fight."

"Asshole, if you wanted to make it look like you put up a fight, then I should have smacked you across the head."

"Um. You're right," agreed Rich. "Here. Take my gun."

I was about to swing the pistol when Rich held up his hand.

"Wait a second. Instead of you hitting me…"

Rich pulled a red capsule from his jacket pocket.

"Got this when we jailed Mary-Kate Olsen for almost hitting a number of celebrities at the Emmys."

He placed the capsule in his mouth, biting into it causing a shot of blood-like liquid to flow from the corner of his mouth.

"Cool, huh?"

"I guess."

He then knelt on the ground.

"Get out of here!" Rich demanded.

Still perplexed, I ran to my car and once my seat belt was secure, I floored it.

CHAPTER FORTY-ONE

Can't Think of a Decent Chapter Title

Still not clear where I needed to go next, I came to a narrow, single lane dirt path. About a half mile down, I hit a fork in the road which kicked up onto my windshield along with a matching spoon and butter knife.

Now I know that might seem like a clunky pun. If only it was that simple an explanation. Deep in thought I had taken my eyes off the road, checking for texts on my cell phone. You've seen enough television commercials and billboards (which ironically you need to take your eyes off the road to read), to know that reading texts while driving is incredibly dangerous. But the fact that at the time of this event texting had yet to be an operational function on cell phones, my blunder was both unsafe as well as implausible.

Failing to notice the split in the road, I rammed the car straight into the grassy divide tossing a tremendous clump of ground in the air that practically buried the entire car. Not so funny. Curious, but not funny.

I couldn't budge my driver side door nor open the window. Luckily, there was a bottle of one hundred proof Ron Rico rum in the glove compartment. If anything would help me forget how bad a situation I was in, it was RR100.

(Two hours later)

I stared at that bottle for what must have been two hours. With over fifteen years of Alcoholics Anonymous soberly tucked deep in my belly, I knew that no matter what proof and how momentarily delightful the rum, drinking from that bottle would not solve my problems.

Maybe just a sip.

(Two more hours)

"Where the fuck am I? Why didn't I call my sponsor?"

I looked down at the bottle. It was empty. Shoot. And my pants were soaked. I must have emptied that bottle and pee'd myself. That was my standard M.O. Pass out and spray-wiz my clothes. Strange though. The car didn't have that rich urine ambiance.

I rubbed my pants leg and took a good whiff of my hand. Oops. Wrong hand. I sniffed the correct hand. Rum. Not urinated rum. Just plain ole rum.

I must've fallen asleep just as I opened the bottle. I wasn't drunk. I was drenched in rum. One hundred proof rum.

I couldn't budge the car forward. I slid the gear into reverse and still, nothing.

"Bonjour. Est quelqu'un dans là?" I heard from someone outside. As you know, I didn't understand French but I knew when someone wanted to know if anyone was buried alive under a small mountain of dirt.

"Yes," I yelled. "I'm an American who is in the car buried under the dirt!"

"I'm sorry I don't understand English," he said in English.

"But that is English."

"Yes. but I only know how to say 'I'm sorry I don't understand English' and 'Yes, But I only know how to say ...'"

Obviously, I believe that readers love when you drill the same a joke into the ground.

"Just get me out of here!"

"Mais je vais creuser vous sortir de là."

I didn't know what he said but I could hear the digging.

Finally, I would be free.

While he continued to dig, I had a revelation. This saving humanity was something I was not suited for. When I'm freed from this Tesla prison I will head back to the States and try to start my life anew.

I didn't think I could ever talk anyone into believing that I did or did not kill Larry. Could I be sure he was even dead? I mean how many false alarms could he sound? And with Ztivo and O'Reilly hunting me down, it would probably be best if I would just move to some cool Midwestern bachelor pad where no one knew me (similar to Hollywood). There I would find a greeting job at a Walmart or perhaps writing for a 7-11. Not at a producer level. Staff writer would be fine.

Finally, I heard a knock on the moon roof. The electric switch wouldn't work. I found a tire iron in the emergency tire iron compartment and attempted to pry open the hatch. It wouldn't budge.

"I can't budge it," I yelled.

"Mouvement de la voie!" insisted my would-be rescuer.

"I don't understand."

"Move into the fuckin' back seat!"

I guessed there are certain phrases that are universal.

I climbed into the back seat.

Like Mike Tyson putting his fist through Mother Theresa's jaw, an arm came through the moon roof knocking it clean off its tracks allowing a shitload of dirt to pour through.

"Grab my hand," he urged.

"I'm sorry. I don't understand French."

"Grab my fucking hand!"

"That was English!"

"I guess I do understand."

I grabbed hold of the hand that was more crane shovel than appendage. Not that it was all that large than it was a rich, construction yellow.

I was literally yanked out of my shoes as my emancipator freed me from the oppression of the dirt bondage. I might be overstating the slavery analogy, but believe me, as a middle-class, anxiety-ridden, Jewish writer, this was about as I-understand-what-my-black-brothers-have-gone-through as it gets.

Once I cleared my near grave, I wiped the dirt from my eyes and found myself face to face with my liberator…

MICHAEL ZTIVO!

"Hello, Stephen."

Open-mouthed, I had a difficult time wrapping my brain around what was happening. Here was the man who was probably behind the murder of many of the world's top comedy writers and, most likely, wanted me dead.

"It's Steven, with a 'v'," I clarified.

Mixed feelings swirled through my head. If he was to kill me, while it could be considered a negative, in effect, I would be on a similar stratum as the great writers. A terrific addition to my resume, yet if I was honest with myself, dead is an even worse work-deterrent than ageism.

On the other hand, as an agent, Ztivo had been well-connected for years. He was, in fact, Super-Agent. In another time, another place, I couldn't get within a mile of Ztivo and yet here we were, one on one. In a way it was about as close to as meaningful meeting I could ever have with someone as powerful. I realized that my priorities were a wee bit out of sorts, but before I lost the opportunity, I thought that this might have been the only chance I would have to pitch a person who had – and "had" was the operative word – mucho heat.

He snapped a pair of handcuffs on me. Inexplicably, he placed both cuffs on the same wrist.

"Ahem," I said, nodding towards the cuffs. Really, if you're going to use handcuffs, use them correctly.

Angrily, Ztivo rearranged the cuffs so that it made it difficult to pull my hands apart, or, for that matter, drive most heavy machinery with any proficiency. Handcuffs used properly are like narcotics.

"Better," I said, hoping that my encouragement might get on his better side, that is, if he had one of those sides.

He grabbed me by the collar and nearly sling-shotted me into the back seat of his car. My pitch possibilities were rapidly being replaced by how it felt to be the object du jour on *Cops*. I started practicing, "This is my friend's grandmother's car. I left my license in my pet iguana. Don't look in the trunk."

Ztivo jumped into the front seat and floored it. My neck snapped back. Curiously, it seemed to relieve the muscle spasm that had kept me from sleeping comfortably for nearly fifteen years. So, it was true. Good can come from bad. I had always thought of that as one of those bullshit Facebook profundities that so-called *friends* would toss at you after you posted something personally and emotionally horrific. Say, like having to fake happiness for another writer who was hired for a gig that you had thought you had nailed. Not that I didn't want a friend to get a job, but really, he already sold three free-lance scripts and a pilot in the past year. Where's the fair?

"Shut up," Ztivo bellowed.

Oh my God. I had said all the jealousy crap out loud and did it without the benefit of a single quote (") mark. Was I so grammatically deaf that I couldn't hear what I was saying? Or was I just that unaware of how loud I think?

"Mr. Ztivo. Where are we going?"

"If you don't shut up, wherever we're going, you won't make it there alive."

As many logistical holes that ran through his threat, I thought it would be best that I go with shutting up.

CHAPTER FORTY-TWO

On the Way to Mandalay

O'Reilly, his face so swollen you'd never be able to tell he was the same guy who settled a plethora of sexual harassment charges for over ten million dollars, drove through the backroads of suburban Paree. Frank Rich, sat in the passenger seat, head in hand, fake blood running down his chin.

"Where are we going?" asked Rich.

"Well, not Mandalay."

Shit. I'll need to come up with another chapter name before the next printing.

"We're going to the one place we should have headed to in the first place."

"Where's that?"

"When we first interrogated Young, what did he say?"

"A lot of crazy, but extremely unfunny, bullshit."

"Right. But that crazy bullshit might have just been the information that could lead us to his hideout."

"Uh… Yeah. What crazy bullshit was that?"

"Remember he said he was a big fan of Art Carney, Jerry Lewis and Lou Costello?"

"Sort of, but…"

"C'mon. You're supposed to be a detective."

"Well, I'm a better writer."

"Well, start thinking like a detective."

"I'm lost."

"Jerry Lewis. Where was he big?"

"Hollywood?"

"And…"

"Las Vegas?"

"France, Schmuck. The French love Lewis. At least they did."

"Okay…"

"And Art Carney."

"What about Art Carney?"

"His name was Art."

"Yes. Yes it was. So what?"

"So what? Art? Are you that thick? Where do you find art in France?"

"Everywhere?"

"Does his mention of LOU Costello not mean anything to you?"

"Short. Somewhat overweight. Hysterical. The entire 'Hey, Abbott!' thing… maybe a bit overdone, but still funny. It was a different time and…"

"Asshole!" O'Reilly interrupted angrily, which I guess is an unnecessary description since he used the term "asshole," along with my inclusion of an exclamation mark (!). "His name was LOU Costello."

After a dumbfounded pause from Rich.

"French. Art. Where do you find French art? At the Lou."

"That means bathroom."

"Schmuck. It's Lou as in Louvre. It all comes together."

"Oh-kay."

With the same oomph that he *did it live* at Inside Edition, O'Reilly floored it, his rear tires sprayed a dirt shower onto a sign post that read, "Louvre 12 KM – This Way."

CHAPTER FORTY-THREE

Fast Times at Paris High

The French countryside sped by like a 45RPM record running backwards at 78RPM (still running thin on contemporary similes/metaphors). I closed my eyes to keep from the fast-approaching return of the nausea reading in the car brought on when I was eleven.

I tried to think of something to keep my mind focusing on whatever impending danger I was sure to face – not unlike my failed attempts to slow down my rapidly oncoming orgasms by thinking of legendary sports events. Unfortunately, being a sports enthusiast, most of those events were more sensual to me than the sexual episodes I was involved in, even when someone else was participating. It didn't matter whether I was thinking about the legend of Babe Ruth pointing his bat to where he was going to hit a home run (which he was purported to do) or the video-supported thirty-seven points Klay Thompson of the Golden State Warriors scored in a single quarter (which he did do). The point is that my inner-thinking ploy usually worked the opposite of what I wanted to accomplish and here I was trying the same thing.

Clearly, I'm an idiot.

So, I thought about what an alcoholic would do in my situation. Not that I am an alcoholic but I have this friend who is. Pretty close friend. I, I mean he, would always say that he wasn't in control of how things happen, that it's all in a higher power's hands. If there was a higher power that's in control, then I would have had no power of what was going to happen. To many that might give some peace in that you didn't have to think about what actions you might have taken to change an outcome. What bothered me was the physical and emotional pain I would feel no matter who was in control.

A lot of people go to their death kicking and screaming. Then there are others who accept the outcome which takes away much of the fear of death. Problem is, unless you were given sufficient morphine, who knows what agony you'll go through? If the end came in your sleep, alright. Not bad. But what if you're captured by terrorists or some other psychotic? They could create some kind of slow, torturous punishment. You know… pulling off your fingernails … and maybe your toenails too. Then, they could start cutting off appendages. Most likely, a good number of people would pass out. But what if they gave you so many uppers or Diet Coke with caffeine so that there would be no way you could faint? Then you'd feel everything. Really, I don't care who's in control, getting your appendages cut off smarts – not to mention watching the blood spurting out from your nubs. Plain nauseating.

So instead, I decided to pray to God, if there was one, to let my death be a quick one. Then it hit me. If God could make my death quick, why shouldn't I shoot for the big one – God not having me die at all? And while He was at it, why not just let me completely off the hook? Let me be free to live my life, have a couple million dollars and a three-picture deal.

At that very moment a lightning bolt – from a cloudless sky – hit the car sending us into a counter-clockwise spin.

My guess was that there was a decent possibility that if there wasn't a God, weather had some great timing.

"Holy shit," yelled Ztivo as he struggled to keep the car from spiraling off the road.

I closed my eyes seeking some sort of escape. I was never one for walking through feelings. You know, feeling them. Instead, drinking, drugging, Etch-a-Sketch were my go-tos to forget about life for a while. I would have written *Piano Man* but a severe lack of musical talent and Billy Joel and Bernie Taupin's's ability to publish it before I had the chance to write it were just a couple of obstacles that life placed in my way. Sexual distractions were good for two to three minutes, but fantasies were getting harder and harder to think of and having others participate created more anxiety than life's curveballs even if I could come up with the money.

I mean, life throws you a lot of curve balls. I remember my first menage-a-troix. The other two never showed up but you have to work with what gets thrown at you.

About the only consistent life avoidance that worked was sleep. My go-to-sleep television shows were usually reruns of *Seinfeld* or *CSI Levittown (PA)*. Even with my eyes closed I could picture every scene.

I closed my eyes and let nature take its course. But first I got a flaccid reminder why sex was a nonstarter.

CHAPTER FORTY-FOUR

Syndicated Escape

While it wasn't my favorite episode, what first came to mind was the one written around the recently-deceased Jimmy. You know – the sneakers sales guy – who always spoke in the third person until O'Reilly kilt him dead. Larry could take what might have been a single thought, exaggerate it and mold it into a sitcom character like no other. There might have been a bit of an overstatement here as every sitcom character seems to be built around his or her embellished personality and fatal flaws. But for a sitcom that a great deal of the time bore some semblance to real life, Seinfeld's character depictions were magnified many-fold and shoved hilariously down your throat.

Since I have taught business writing I had used that episode as an example of how writing in the third person distances people from one another. Really. How distracting. How pompous. Still, it was funny.

I soon found myself moving quickly through episodes and characters.

When I got to the *The Contest*, where the foursome bet each other on who could go the longest without masturbating, my standard thought-process approach was to focus on Elaine (Dreyfus). Actually anything in *Seinfeld* that dealt with anything sexual, similar to her role in *The Sponge*, where a limited amount of contraceptive sponges led Elaine to judge every man based on his *sponge-worthiness*, I was fixated on how much I was attracted to Elaine. Even when she was written to appear clumsy or dumb or somehow unappealing, to me she became, not unattractive, but adorable. Of course, if there would the possibility of a relationship with Elaine, no matter how fictional, I'm sure it wouldn't take long before that adorableness turned into annoyance.

But she was so cute.

And as soon as I went there, boom, sex reemerged as a short but memorable distraction. And, as customary, sleep soon followed.

Followed by dreams.

As dreams are wont to do, I found myself wandering through the *Seinfeld* episodes in a place of the character mixed up with some mish-mosh drawn from my own life.

I stepped out of a pool and found myself naked in front of a number of attractive pig boys. My *shrinkage* was obvious. Devastatingly, there was no water in the pool. I placed on my fluffy pirate shirt to feed my horse a Costco barrel of beans as I ran with my virgin, naked housekeeping, Miss America contestant girlfriend named Dolores even though I wanted to sleep with Elaine again. But dammit, she was dating my newly-minted Jewish, close-talking dentist as well as the guy who also did the voice of Joe in *Family Guy*.

I don't remember the rest.

CHAPTER FORTY-FIVE

Lourving Art

I was awakened by the sweet melodious tones of serenity.

"Fucking traffic," growled Ztivo.

I peeked outside the window to see a large glass pyramid. Many people who were less aware of the evidence surrounding the Wonders of the World might have thought we were in Egypt. But, come on, folks. It was late in the evening, yet you could see there was no sand surrounding this Pyramid. This was not Egypt. This had to be Vegas.

Upon a closer examination I found that the surrounding area was discernably free of hookers and excessively short t-shirts exposing excessively overhanging bellies. It was not like anyone would forget their second-grade cartography placemats. It became clear we were creeping slowly on the Rue d Rivoli. That could only mean one thing. We were about to arrive at the Louvre in Paris.

♪Dun-dun.♫*64

Ztivo pulled into an indoor parking lot around the corner of the Lourve. He drove to the bottom level and pulled into a space.

"Where…?" which was about all I could get out of my mouth before he dragged me from the car with one tug.

"Shut up!"

64 *Thank you, Dick Wolf*

With a large pistol dug into the center of my back, he walked me to a wall. He banged on the wall nine times. Wait, no. It was eight times. The ninth time he stopped just short of the wall.

"Was it eight or nine times?" Ztivo mumbled, more to himself than asking for my input.

Just then a section of the wall, maybe two feet wide by five feet high, slid open.

Ztivo pushed me in. I didn't duck down enough, thereby getting my head slammed into the top of the opening.

"Watch your head" warned Ztivo.

"Great timing," I whimpered.

After about a hundred yards being pushed through ankle-high sludge I realized we were in the bowels of the Lourve. Dead giveaway was the arrow just before a sign that read, "Lourve." Ztivo continued to shove me down a long, dark and dank hallway – more dank than dark.

Now I'm six foot, about 185 pounds, despite what my doctor's scale reads. I've long believed there is a direct link between doctors' scales and/or mirrors (most of which have no idea what I truly look like) and weight-loss corporations. Pretty much, reality adds about twenty-five pounds. That'll send most people to some quick fix purchase or a psychologist who isn't on your insurance plan. Not me. Half a peach half once a week… I'm good.

He opened a door and we found ourselves inside the world famous Lourve.

I always wanted to go there, even writing a number of screenplays that took place in Paris, especially in the Lourve, so that I could write off any visit I made to France. That I never sold any of those scripts, nor had the money to make the trip in the first place, remained a barrier.

Being that it was after hours there were no visitors, one could not escape the utter beauty of the paintings and sculptures that populated the rooms.

"Why are we here?" I asked.

"I think that will be obvious very shortly."

"I could be jumping to conclusions, but if there is the slightest chance that you brought me here to take in the fine art, would you mind if I could check out the Mona Lisa?"

"Are you serious?"

"Please."

Ztivo's pistol dug deep into my back.

"Is that a yes?"

"Yeah. Sure."

WHOMP!

That was a swift knock across the back of my head, sending me to the floor. While the pain was apparent, what was also apparent was that from my angle on the floor, I caught a view of a section of a wall that held a painting of an almost-smiling, unattractive woman.

THE MONA LISA!

That Mona Lisa. Not one of my films was produced and yet here I was, albeit lying on the floor, dripping blood, looking right at The Mona Lisa and I wasn't charged a cent. Of course,

There was a strong chance it would cost my life.

Still… The Mona Lisa.

It was protected by a glass cover. Smart. If it wasn't there I know it would be difficult for me not to touch her/it.

Ztivo lifted me up by the collar. His favorite way of standing me up.

"The Mona Lisa," I pointed it out to Ztivo as if he had no idea that it was the Mona Lisa.

Ztivo ignored me as he pulled out some sort of rod, extending it some twenty feet which he used to push a point high up on the wall above the legendary lady. After a moment the case along with the painting creaked away from the wall, revealing another hallway.

Jesus, Lourve must be the French word for "secret passages."

"Get goin," said Ztivo.

With his pistol placed strategically between my scapulars I was shoved through the opening. Almost immediately we came up to a four-teen-foot high, gold encrusted, triple door. A double door would have been enough, but it is well known that the French have always thought more is better… except in restaurant serving size. Ztivo knocked four and a half times. After some ten seconds, more like eleven, a small hatch in the door opened, barely exposing a pair of swollen eyes and a narrow, boney nose.

"What do you want?" asked the eyes and nose I assumed belonged to more of a face.

"I'd like to go back home," I said. "Hollywood, per se. Anything in that general area. Even Sherman Oaks adjacent would be acceptable."

Ztivo yanked me up high enough to force a choking sound that I didn't think I was capable of – halfway between a wounded elk and a wounded elk who had access to a bullhorn. He lifted me high enough so that the guard could see me.

"What's that?" asked the guard.

"He's the person who knows more than he should," said Ztivo.

The guard's face grimaced. I could see his eyes fill with blood, blood as red as the deepest red blood (you may think similes are easy, but you're kind of limited to words like *like* or *as* or *so* or *than* or some verbs like *resemble*. Then again, you want to tell me that Wikipedia isn't information gold).

"I can see that you're extremely busy and I'd be the last person who'd want to add to your workload…"

WHACK!

That was as close to the description of the sound a watermelon makes when a Gallagher-type mallet was slammed into it. I could feel the seeds shoot out from my nose.

"Shut your freak'n mouth," Ztivo thundered.

"Wait a minute. You're a homicidal machine who uses the word 'fuck' like it needs to babysit every other word out of your mouth and now you say, 'Shut your FREAK'N mouth?' What the hell is that about?"

CLUNK!

Which is the sound my head makes when the butt of a rifle slams against it while you try to clarify some obviously questionable slang usage.

The doors slowly creaked open and Ztivo escorted/dragged me into a large, cavernous room. More cavern than room. Like the inside of a cave and just as cold. Long icicles hung from the ceiling, ones that would have taken hundreds of years to form.

On the wall was the inscription, "Sigilum Militum Xpisti." In parentheses following were the words, "Seal of the Army of Christ." Obviously, these guys were concerned with English-speaking tourism. More likely, they were part of Knights Templar.

At the end of the room sat a long, wide wooden table. If I knew my wood, I'd say wine-soaked mahogany. Probably elderberry. A French domestic or an American transnational depending what land you're standing on when you're standing on it.

All the chairs were empty except the one at the far end. That chair was taller than all the others. Almost a throne. Yet as magnificent as the chairs were, I didn't sense the slightest hint of an aroma of wine. Not elderberry. Not plum. Not even cherry. Neither foreign nor domestic. Yet there was something. Something familiar. Sweet but not wine sweet. It harkened back to my days growing up in the Ozarks. Not the mountains. Ozarks Estates, a condo village nestled in the back woods of Studio City. My friends and I would gather round the old-metal-coal barbeque firing up short ribs, the shortest ribs you could ever imagine. So short that from one end to another you couldn't measure it. At that time technology had yet been developed to decipher a distance that small without tearing a hole so large in the exosphere that if you were driving a 70,000 pound tandem axle tractor trailer across the exosphere it would slip easily through that hole without ever coming near the sphere's edge. Clean through, I tellya.

Southern Comfort!

That was it. Fuckin' Southern Comfort. That chair's wood had been soaked in Southern Comfort liquor. Not the mamby-pamby, high school kid eighty-six proof. I'm talking the hundred proof that hits you where you live. Unless, of course, if you live in either Iowa or South Dakota. Punks!

Climbing out of a large, smoking hole in the floor – that appeared to be a chasm leading out of hell – came men and women who I couldn't name due to the possible litigious complications, and probably even more important, I didn't know their names. What I had no problem recognizing was what each of them stood for. Unable to hide their alliances smacking of outrageous ego, they each wore oversized labels that illustrated their connected factions. Wall Wall Street, Power Companies, Television Programming Executives, Radio Talk Show Hosts, Advertising, Politics, Multi-billion Dollar Corporations, Big Pharma, Big Oil, Banks, the Industrial Military Complex, Skinny Jeans, Food Additives, Television Talk Shows, Disney and others who chose much smaller fonts too difficult to read.

Were they wearing labels? Not much of a fashion statement. Or was it that they weren't so much labels as what they were was written on their faces. Yup, upon closer inspection it was written in deep red Sharpie ink. And I don't think it was washable.

They were the most powerful of the most powerful people in the world. Of course, power here was signified not by who they were but what they represented.

NRA reps were busy handing out association applications along with personalized silver bullets.

They began to chant….

"Si-i-i-i-i-it…

Ri-i-i-i-ight…

Ba-a-a-a-ck…

A-n-n-n-nd…

We-e-e-e'll…

Te-e-e-e-ell…

A-a-a-a-a-a…

Ta-a-a-a-ale…

A-a-a-a-a-a…

Ta-a-a-a-ale…

O-o-o-o-of…

A-a-a-a-a-a…

Fa-a-a-a-te…

Fu-u-u-u-ul…

Tri-i-i-i-i-ip…"

In the chair/throne at the far end of the table was a man I didn't recognize. He was sixty, maybe sixty-two years old with finely sculptured G.I. Joe cheek bones. More plastic than cartilage. On second thought, he could have been in his late sixties. With recent upgrades to cosmetic surgery and again, Cher's ability to look like a solid ten at eighty years of age you never know. This guy could have been in his early nineties.

He had to be over two and a half meters tall if he were an inch and a half. Of course, he was sitting so I could only surmise that his visible upper body was resting atop a comparably-sized lower torso along with sufficient leggage. Precisely how tall he was based on a sparse recall of my high school anatomy class, so I wouldn't bet on it.

He appeared to be financially secure. Some might say wealthy. Others might call him well healed. It really depended on how extensive the thesaurus one would typically access. He wore a finely-tailored, double-breasted, pin-striped suit. I guessed he was a Hollywood agent, the kind who didn't return phone calls unless his client had a three-picture deal. 'Course he could have been a lawyer, one who represented agents or writers with three picture deals. Suffice it to say: great suit.

Whatever his profession I was pretty sure he was an evil villain of some sort. In his lap sat a large white Persian cat in hen-position that he petted slowly, but purposely. A dead villain giveaway. All he'd have to do is place his pinky in his mouth for me to… Oh, my god! Pinky heading straight for the mouth! Oh, never mind, he was just wiping a little schmutz from the corner of his mouth.

Ztivo picked me up by the collar a flung me down the slick, well-waxed table where I slid like a mug of draft beer down to a drunk at the other end of the bar. Not a drop spilt. I came to a stop some eleven inches from the agent/lawyer person.

"Sit down, Mr. Young," he said with your standard used-car salesman smile, as his cat gave me one of those "I'm better than you" looks. See, this is why I'm not a cat guy. Cats. They think they're so hot.

I climbed tentatively from the table into a chair next to my new *friend*. He knew my name. I didn't know if that was good or bad. I didn't know if the smile was friendly or the first salvo of a con.

"Mr. Young. May I call you 'Steven'?"

"I suppose so, as long as you say it with a 'v' and not a 'ph.'"

"Certainly."

I felt I had just won the first battle, albeit only a spelling victory. Steven vs Stephen doesn't sound much different from one another, but really, what Steven wants his name to be pronounced Stephen.

"Stephen…"

"Steven," I corrected.

"Steven," he said accurately. "Do you know why you're here?"

"Sure. Because Godzilla here chased me…"

SMACK!

Ztivo slammed me up one side of my face…

SMACK!

…and down the other. He did so with such force I was surprised my head stayed connected to my neck.

"Thank you for your service, Michael," said the sharp dresser. "Your work here is finished. Cheers."

"You're most welcome, my sage." said Ztivo with a slight bow and an almost cartoonish triple-flip of his hand.

From under the table the sharp dresser pulled a Smith & Wesson .44 Magnum Revolver, the same one used by Clint Eastwood in *Dirty Harry*, except this one was not fictional (well a little). Before Ztivo could react, he was drilled by a perfectly placed bullet into the center of his forehead. Ztivo dropped lifelessly into a pool of his own bright, thick, almost fluorescent, plasma. Surprisingly, instead of the expected red, the color of his blood was blue. A deep sky blue. Ztivo was a legitimate blue blood.

Interesting.

But wow. This was a cold (albeit blue)-blooded murder of someone who, arguably, was once the most powerful person in show business. It was at that point that I noticed a wet spot on the front of my pants. Not the standard wet spot I inadvertently embarrassed myself every so often. Of course, I was excited at the moment but come on. Being the spot was blue,

I realized that it was just collateral body fluid from Ztivo's wound. In reality it was Ztivo who should have been embarrassed, though it didn't seem like an immediate concern to him.

"You just murdered him!" I exclaimed.

"I don't know if I would go so far as to call it, 'murder.'"

"You shot him."

"Well, you have me there. But, let's be honest, just because you shoot a person doesn't mean they have to die. I can give you plenty of evidence that will illustrate that most people who had been shot, survived."

He opened a laptop and began to tap on the keyboard.

"You don't have to prove to me…"

"No, I don't want you thinking that I'm some kind of homicidal killer when…"

"I get it. I get it."

He turned the laptop screen towards me.

"See. Wikipedia doesn't lie."

"Okay. You're not a murderer."

"Do you know who I am?" asked the supposed *non-killer* with the still smokin' pistol in his grasp.

"No idea."

Thought that it might help to be proactive.

"Do you want me to guess?"

"Not necessary. There are many who know me as 'Master.' Those who are closest to me call me 'Da Vinci.'"

"Leonardo?"

His smile grew, more smirk than smile.

"Very funny, Steven. No. My first name is Da."

"Yu-uh. Okay, Da. Why am I here? What do you want from me?"

"I think you misunderstand. It's not me who wants you here. It's really your country that NEEDS you here."

"I don't understand. For the past week I've been jailed, shot at, chased across the ocean and dragged through the countryside while a bunch of great comedy writers were being murdered. If that weren't bad enough everyone seems to be trying to nail those murders on me. How's that mean my country wants me?"

"All will be explained in time. First, let me ask you a question."

"I guess."

"What's the capitol of New Hampshire?"

"I don't know. Concord?"

"Correct." Now let me ask a third question."

"Excuse me, but this would be the second question."

"I'll get to that in time. My question is based on the fact that you had once stated, and I'm paraphrasing here… that if a whole bunch of successful comedy writers died, you'd be in a good position to get a job. In fact you might even be able to have your own show."

"It was a joke."

"Doesn't seem very funny to me."

"Yeah, well. It wasn't so much of a joke as a statement of frustration."

"Exactly. And that brings me to why you're here."

Finally.

He stood up, walked around to my back and began to rub my clavicle as well as my nearby scapula similarly to how former President George W. Bush attempted to massage former German Chancellor Merkel's shoulders. While Bush's move was considered by many to be inappropriate, and while it was kind of weird, Bush was only trying to relax Merkel.

"I represent a consortium that for years has been here to protect society from those who want to appropriate the minds of the public under the guise of literal truths."

"A little to the left," I interrupted.

"What? Oh, sure."

While the entire episode was especially strange it didn't hurt to take advantage of the situation. Similarly, when you're in prison on trumped up charges and your cellmate offers to give you a back rub. You are not going to turn down Bubba. If you think you would then you have no idea how stressful a day in the yard can be.

"As I was saying," he continued, "the public, left to their own devices, could be swayed by these virtual outlaws, who in their own sordid interest, throw around actual facts, accurate figures and quality work in an attempt to deceive."

"First of all, a little to the right," I directed to him to hit the spot that not only caused many a sleepless night, but I'm convinced it kept me from a very solid Major League Baseball career. "Yeah. Yeah." I purred. "That's it."

"We feel that someone like you would understand the import of giving our country simple concepts and repetitive programming that would neither make audiences feel stupid, tax their thinking nor frustrate the viewing public in a manner that, quite honestly, is un-American."

"I'm not exactly sure what you're trying to say. It almost seems like you're stating, and might I add, quite eloquently, that the reason you're speaking to me is that I don't write very well."

"Ah, that almost sounds like the reaction of a person who is more interested in his own ego than the well-being of society. That's not at all the Steve Young I know."

"You know me?"

"Very well."

"How? I mean, I don't know you."

"All you have to know about me is that I am a patriotic American who cares that we, as a country, don't end up harming our children and our children's children."

"But how would…?"

"The children," Vinci interrupted.

"But…"

"Children."

"B…"

"And their children. I mean the potential hardship could end up affecting children forever. I think we might be looking at the possibility we may not be able to have children altogether.

"What? How…?

"Pregnancy itself could end up going the way of the Panda Bear."

"The Panda Bear isn't extinct."

"Yet," said Vinci.

Yet. I love that word. You could use it as the perfect rebuttal to almost any argument. And when I say any argument, I mean *any*.

"There's no way you can prove that the Earth is only 6,000 years old."

"Yet."

See. That doesn't even make any sense yet it's very hard to deny.

"Steven, would you want to place your children in a toxic world where a bunch of socialist elitists control their autoimmune systems? Many scientists – not necessarily many – but more than one – maybe not exactly more than one – but there was a guy at the Heritage Foundation who created a study – a photocopy of a study – that confirms this to be absolutely true, so I'm sure you can…."

I didn't interrupt. He just stopped speaking and squinted a laser stare that could have drilled a hole through my head and into the person standing in back of me. I waited a couple beats, but figured if I didn't say something soon the awkward silence would have grown even more uncomfortable and anxious.

Anxiety has been my constant companion since my first relationship breakup in second grade. In first grade I was considered a hot ticket. All the girls at Beth Moyle would plead to share their milk and kugel with me. I got cocky. I thought that I had it made until second grade when I was regularly going out to recess with 2nd grade fox, Sharon Sharone. I go to get a reservation on the swings and the next thing I know she's on the slide in the lap of third grade mathletic whiz, Aaron Avonowitzberg. That was it. Confidence blown and it became the commencement of an angst that would wake me up and rock me to sleep every night for the rest of my life.

Anxiety doesn't feel great, but you get used to it. Like a lengthy marriage or a neighborhood restaurant, you know your partner will be there every morning and she might not be poisoning your food, but it doesn't mean you wouldn't prefer to dine at a more fuckable restaurant.

I had to break the silence.

"First of all, that last sentence you said meant nothing. It wasn't even a complete sentence. I have no idea what you're talking about."

"And that's exactly the point. It makes no sense to continue to allow these anarchists to diminish the people's ability and might I add, God-given right to understand what they want to do with their life, and more important, what they want to spend their money on."

"Wait, wait, wait. You're talking about what Richard Lewis and Larry David told me."

"Anarchists," mumbled the harrumphing herd of lowlife elites.

"Larry, ava shulum, was right. You guys want creative talent to stop writing clever material for television. You want to use television, especially sitcoms, to *dumb down* America."

"Mr. Young, you misunderstand. It is not only me who believes in you. If you look around this room you will see the people, who with their position and clout, are interested in standing behind you and your talent to create material that will entertain the American public for years. They know your, um, artistic ability to write programming will be easily grasped by hundreds of millions of working Americans who don't need to have to engage in some energy-draining thought-process after a hard day at work."

"You're basically saying that I write crap."

"Don't sell yourself short."

"How else can I take it? You're saying you want someone to write lousier scripts."

"Not lousier. Simpler.

"Yeah, that's just perfect."

"And not really simple, because after a short time, with no perplexing, complex writing distracting audiences, your work will be what audiences will see as… as… as the best there is."

"Yeah, well without any competition then they'll also see me as the worst."

"That's where we step in, Mr. Young," said a gorgeous, female tobacco executive wearing a form-fitting $5,000 suit that shouted privilege, intellect and sex. The sex emanated from a most-likely, purposeful nip-slip.

"Steven, audiences will look on you as a compelling voice for the people. Seriously, with everyone else out the way you will be the one the public will look to, not only for entertainment but to be a voice for them. You're a true outsider. You wouldn't be adding more slop to the entertainment swamp. In effect, you'd be draining the swamp."

I noticed of few of the narcissistic businessmen taking notes… one orange-haired attendee in particular.

You'd be like Walter Cronkite or Jon Stewart or Derek Jeter but without having the need to read."

"What do you mean, without the 'need to read?'"

"Your opinion will be enough," she said sensually as she licked the side of my face from my jawline to the top of my ear. "You won't have to be learned."

"Learned?"

"Learn-ned."

"Ah."

"It's all good."

"That's good? It still doesn't seem like a good reason for me to get involved."

"If you're the one in charge, that power eliminates the need for reason."

I just stared, not a hundred percent sure what she meant. I mean, I was pretty sure because Richard Lewis told me the exact same thing: "If you're the one in charge, that power eliminates the need for reason."

And when Lewis said it, he didn't mean it as a positive. Still, when presented with this kind of opportunity one needs to weigh the pros and cons. I mean, these – couldn't think of a good word to describe them but not wanting to risk burning bridges in case we did do business in the future, I'll just go with "not nice" – not nice people would be the only ones who would know what I did. The rest of the world would think I was some-one at the top of my game. They might even look at me as resurrecting an industry that had been decimated by the deaths of so many of the giants. As an extra benefit, I'd hit the lottery financially. I'd be sitting pretty, set up for life. There would be a reserved "Steve Young" table at the Ivy. My wife would be thrilled and if not, options for other wives and girlfriends would be wide open, though probably not. My wife has always been ada-mant about keeping my happiness at bare minimum. Sure, I'd be someone with zero integrity, but who needs integrity when you have wealth beyond your dreams. Shit, it would hopefully be wealth beyond my nightmares. I have far more nightmares than I have dreams.

I sat there leaning towards fame, fortune and although fallacious, the appearance of respectability.

Yet questions kept creeping in.

How would I be able to sleep, albeit in a luxurious mansion in Bel Air? Probably very well and if not, that's what Lorazepam is for. But when I'd wake up how could I look at myself in the mirror? Well, I could rid my home of every mirror or, for that matter, any piece of reflective material.

"Well, Steve?" asked Vinci.

"I'm thinking, I'm thinking," I said, once again borrowing from Mr. Benny.

In actuality, I was thinking. I may not have been successful based on the amount of money I made or in getting my own shows on the air, but when I wrote there were those times when I wrote well. There isn't one person in my family, other than my wife, who said anything less. That was the one thing I was most proud of. Of course, in the end it would always be a subjective matter. Still, while I was inspired by the greats of writing, I was confident and proud that my work was original. I never went into a writing session with any other mindset than coming up with something new, clever and what I hoped would make audiences laugh. Damn it, I won on *The Gong Show.*[65]* There was only one Steve Young, except for the one who wrote for Letterman and okay, the one who was a country singer, and of course, the Hall of Fame quarterback for the San Francisco Forty Niners. Probably tens of thousands more. But not one of them were me… that I know of.

"Would I be able to write about the impending danger from climate change?" I asked.

"Sure, Steven," said Da. "You can write fiction."

"Um. You're saying climate change is fiction?"

---

65 *I won with a ventriloquism act. I don't know how to ventriloquiz.*

"Of course."

"Come on. There's no legitimate evidence to refute the existence of global warming."

"Yet."

"What? Are you saying that the 97% of scientists who claim here is climate change are wrong?"

"Yet."

"That doesn't even make sense."

"Yet."

See. It really works.

"But if you want to write about climate change being affected by manmade activities, you can."

"Wow. Great."

"But… we'll need to have to stamp the word, 'fiction' on the episode."

"On the script?"

"On the screen."

"There'll be a mark on the screen during show?"

"If you consider the word 'FICTION' stamped across the entire screen a 'mark,' sure."

The more I thought about it the more I realized that no matter the level of success I had, what would always be most important was who I was. As bullshitty as that might sound, no matter what others thought of me, it was what I thought of myself that really counted. What was the right thing? Not only what was best for me, but what was the right thing even if I didn't directly benefit from it? On that basis there was only one thing I could have said.

"Nope."

"What?!" exclaimed Vinci.

I took a deep breath.

"You know, sometimes you surprise yourself. I'm not exactly sure why it took this wild ride, a ride all the way to Paris *66 to make me see who I am becoming and how it's someone I don't want to be. Sometimes I guess you need to hit bottom before you see how low you've gone."

"That, Mr. Young, is about as cheesy and elementary an adage as one could come up with," said Vinci. "What's next, a penny saved is a penny earned?"

"Wow," I exclaimed. "A penny saved is a penny earned. That is great. So, if you have a penny but don't spend it – you know, put it into something like a large jar, with suitable air holes, then you've earned it even though you may have just found it. Hold on a second…."

I pulled out my phone to read that quote into it. I've learned from many lost ideas, if you don't do that right away, you'll never remember.

POW!!!

Vinci shot the phone out of my hand.

"Hey! I don't have insurance on that."

Luckily, since I was always dropping my phone, I always carried a spare one.

"Mr. Young. Enough of your rubbish. I just offered you unimaginable power, unlimited cash and the apex of success. Success you would have never been close to receiving from the ghastly scripts you've turned out."

"I'm going to assume that was meant as a compliment."

"You're not turning down the opportunity to become the king of comedy, the premiere sitcom writer on television, are you?"

"First of all, no matter how you try to manipulate the media and the minds of the public to sell your shameful products and corrupt politics, in my heart I will always believe, Larry David is the king of comedy."

---

66 *Another personal tax write-off.*

"You mean, *was* the king," said one who, as best I could remember, was the yet to be elected president by less than fifty percent of the vote, Donald Trump.

I let his words roll around in my head. As much as I lived through Larry's death (both of them), it wasn't until that moment that it hit me – Larry David was gone. We'd no longer be able to appreciate his brilliant take on stories that no other writer would recognize the sumptuous possibilities. They were, as everyone called them, stories about nothing. They were right. They were about nothing… until Larry got a hold of them.

Larry took nothing and squeezed it into diamonds. He was the Superman*[67] of comedy writing. He'd come out of the phonebooth, drawing characters and casting perfect actors who would give flawless voice to his words… perfectly. Every action was drawn to convert a seemingly nothing moment into one that decades (oy) later continued to be laughed at. Try to think of Elaine's awkward-to-a-fault dance and not smile. There was the rumor that those spastic dance moves were taken from SNL Producer Lorne Michaels' actual attempt to dance. But that's just another part of Larry's genius. His eye. Either one of them. He could take ostensibly simple moments and transform them into hysterics. Think Judge Reinhold's *close talker*, George's penis shrinkage, Bryan Cranston's dentist character converting to Judaism "for the jokes." Expressions like "Yada, yada, yada," "sponge-worthy"" and "Not that there's anything wrong with that," landed hysterically into the American lexicon. Really, come December, who doesn't hear someone mention the Jamaican holiday of "Festivus."

There are hundreds more, but the point is it was the absurdist brain of Larry David, the Daniel Webster of comedy writing (and as time-travelers purport, Daniel Webster was the Larry David of enormous brain size), that put it all together into the killer show he and Jerry Seinfeld created.

---

67 *The George Reeves depiction of TV's "Superman" would many times take a lump of coal and squeeze it with such power that it would become a diamond. Well, that's bullshit. Diamonds don't come from coal. No wonder Reeves committed suicide, or so they would like us to think.*

Curb Your Enthusiasm had its own unprecedented take on life. Larry was able to build a show around himself. Lifting your own cringe-worthy life onto the small screen and making it something that every man and a few women could relate to is no easy task. George Burns did a marvelous job of it in the fifties. Shandling in the eighties. George and Gary would have applauded how Larry took their approach and knocked it out of the park.

"Enough of your TV history bullshit!" roared Vinci.

Shit. I kept forgetting not to speak what I was thinking out loud.

"Are you doing this or what?" demanded a rather irate Vinci.

I had a choice which seemed a *live or die* one. I reached into my pocket and pressed "record" on my spare phone. If it worked, this would be all the evidence I'd need.

"But what do I do about every law officer in the world who's looking for me?"

Out of the shadows walked Kevin Spacey. Kevin "Fucking" Spacey. I didn't know his middle name, but there was some talk.

"I'll handle law enforcement… issues Mr. Young," said Spacey with a hint of a Southern drawl. "No need to worry."

"Kevin Spacey?"

I was shocked. Sure, Spacey was a terrific actor but how could he be part of this sordid consortium? And what's with the accent?

"Not Spacey," said Spacey. "Underwood. Frances Joseph Underwood. Spacey is the actor who I no longer associate with. Too much baggage."

"So you're really Frances Underwood?"

I was confused. Frances Underwood was the vile political boss from Netflix's *House of Cards* who Spacey played. Sure, he was a repugnant human being, but he was just a character. A character in a fictional television show.

"I get that you commit to your characters. Sure, you were a decent Bobby Darin, even though you were too old to play Darin. I mean you could have been Sandra Dee's father. But you weren't Bobby Darin. You only played Bobby Darin."

His smile became even more devious.

"Of course I wasn't Bobby Darin. Bobby Darin's dead. Frances Underwood is not dead, yet, Mr. Young."

"Yuh, as a fictional character. He was never alive. He was the figment of Michael Dobb's imagination and that was in a book. Underwood is a television role. It wasn't even an original television role. It was originally a British TV series."

"I see," said Spacey or Underwood. It was getting more confusing by the second. "Is this fictional?"

Out of the same shadows came Robin Wright… NUDE! Completely nude except for a pair of black spiked heels, straps wrapped halfway up her calves.

"Holy… shit," I stuttered.

Okay, she was about fifty-one, but damnit, she was about as hot as, well, as hot as a thirty-seven year old. A naked thirty-seven-year-old who obviously had a trainer.

"Robin Wright?" I stuttered again.

"My wife, Claire Underwood," said the guy I thought was Spacey. "Does she look fictional?"

I could feel a bit of saliva running down the corner of my mouth.

"Um. No… but…"

"Would you like to touch her, Mr. Young?" asked Spa… um, Underwood. "You know, to check if she's… real."

"Go ahead," said a demur, Robin Wri… okay, Claire Underwood. "It's fine with me."

I really, really wanted to. But it was like being at a lingerie fashion show where you're turned on but you have to act like it's no big deal, so it seems like you're totally cool with it.

"Thanks, but I'll pass. I don't know what's happening, but I'll go with it. You guys are Frances and Claire Underwood."

Underwood turned away and broke – I hate to admit this to any thespians with integrity reading this – the fourth wall.

"I do imagine this young man does not believe who I am. That's alright. That just makes my ability to achieve my ends all-the-more promising. I don't even have to reveal my methods. It's like my Father used to tell me. 'Frances, your name is not who you are – it's what you are able to get away with.'"

Underwood turned back to me.

"Son, there isn't a man who can't be persuaded to do what a more powerful man wants him to."

"Anyone?" I asked.

"I just need the names."

His smile grew larger.

"And the names of those closest to them."

Shit.

"Okay. Okay. But I just want to be clear. If I agree, exactly what do you guys get out of this?"

"That's none of your damn business," said Trump. "Hey Da, punch this guy in the face. I'll pay for your attorney."

"Donnie. Not to worry," said Vinci. "It actually gives me great pleasure to explain. If Mr. Young chooses not to take this great opportunity, I'm thinking there's an even greater possibility he won't be around to share it with anyone else. On the other hand, if he chooses to partake in our efforts to make this a *better* world, well, then he's just a part of the family."

A smile crossed Vinci's face. One that evoked the satisfaction one has after sipping a rich chocolate, peanut butter, banana milk shake that is heaped with taste but devoid of calories. I shook with dread that he thought of me as that shake.

"Steven. You are about to join PHLEM, the Priory Hegumes Legion of Extreme Mediocrity. In the past that required a vow of poverty. We've softened the obligation to just 'a vow.' Our predecessors believed our servitude, our Opus Dei, was to suffer as Christ had, but really, that was a little much. I mean, we're children of God, not his sons. So instead, we just try to get as wealthy as possible. Of course, we forgot to tell Ztivo."

"Excuse me," I interrupted. "I appreciate the details, but could you get to the point."

"I don't think you need to know any more than we are giving you the greatest opportunity ever presented to anyone."

I was lost. I didn't know what to do. Yeah, it was a great opportunity, if not so god-damned dishonorable.

"Well, Mr. Young?" pushed Vinci.

Think, think, think. Then, as if someone had removed every fear swirling in my head…

"FUCKING MEDIA!" I blurted out.

"What?" asked Vinci, incredulously.

As if the late Larry David was in charge of my thoughts…

"38-2-54-64-63-34-2," I said softly, repeating Richard Nixon's routine code.

Vinci's face turned ashen.

"NO!!!!" screamed Vinci.

"38-2-54-64-63-34-2," I repeated louder, more powerfully than before.

High up on the wall behind Vinci, a hologram appeared revealing Richard Nixon speaking to his longtime secretary, Rosemary Woods.

Every fiber in my body trembled.

Nixon: Rosemary, are you sure this Oval Office meeting of PHLEM will never see the light of day? Or even more important, the light of our court system.

Woods: As sure as I am that I can stretch my leg halfway across the room to accidentally erase this tape.

Nixon: That's my girl. Boys, and when I say boys I mean John, Bob, Henry, Rupert and all of you captains of industry who head up energy, pharmaceutical, media, tobacco, fast food, food additives, technology and especially advertising and television companies, thank you for all showing up.

All: Hazzah!

Nixon: Gentleman, the oath.

All: (Clearing elderly phlegm-filled throats) I am in charge. I am beautiful. I am the best in the history of the world. Everyone else is less. I am the most important person in the world. I deserve what I want. I can do no wrong. I am right even when I am wrong. God bless us all. And if He chooses not to bless us, really, who cares. Just remember, our will, not His, be done. Amen.

Nixon: Amen. Okay, here's the deal. From the time I debated that little Richie Rich prick Kennedy, it became obvious that there was no more powerful force than television. For crissakes, who knew that my five o'clock shadow would show up closer to noon. Television is the access to the public's living room. The student doesn't learn from a schoolteacher. He learns from the television set. When a teacher tells a girl to study hard to get a good job, but a TV commercial says that smoking Parliament cigarettes will attract a rich husband, which does a girl listen to? Especially when nine out of ten doctors smoke them.

All: (Big guffaws)

Nixon: When you watch young, good-looking people having a great time eating at McDonalds, what chance do healthy choices have? Would you rather eat vegetables in the corner of your sad and lonely kitchen or hang out with the cool, handsome crowd eating great-tasting crap.

Donald Trump: I love crap.

Erlichman: What the hell is this freakin' punk doing here?

Nixon: Easy, John. He may be a kid, but believe me, in thirty-forty years he's going to be so ego-centric, he'll be able to take a prodigious dump on New York City and swear it smells like Hai Karate. We need that kind of hubris to maintain this program.

Trump: I like dumps.

Erlichman: Asshole.

Nixon: The point is when the school years are over, television continues. It's even more profound than religion. When religion preaches killing is bad but TV says we're killing far more Viet Cong than they're killing Americans, whose killing does the public believe is sanctioned by God? Don't short-change its power. Television is a religion. Television and advertising provide the truth that matters: the truth the public wants to believe. The shortcuts that make dreams come true. And why do they believe it? Because stupid is easy and people always want the easy. We need to provide the stupid.

Trump: Here-here.

Erlichman: Shut up, punk.

Nixon: Take it Henry.

Kissinger (in a thick Mississippi drawl): People love to laugh and they believe that television comedy is supposed to make them laugh. We need to make sure that programming is as mindless as possible. That means that from this point on there will be no more than two or three great television programs a decade. If a producer comes up with something unique or smart, he will not be allowed to create another clever program ... ever. If he does, he or his show is to be canceled immediately.

Haldeman: Just to be clear, when you say canceled, do you mean…?

Nixon: Yes. The cutting your throat move you just simulated does suggest what I meant. We need to lower the level of what the public believes to be intelligent. In this way the mediocre will become what is deemed the top of the line and the inferior product will be considered acceptable. Sometimes even exceptional.

Murdoch: Then what you are saying is that the American public will buy any bill of goods we want to sell them.

Nixon: Exactly, Rupe. Like saying I have a plan to exit Viet Nam if I were elected, even though I don't have a plan nor want to pull out at all. Of course, after I'm reelected and we do pull our men out under severe enemy fire we can declare it a "victory." Gentlemen, the benefits to you will blossom as if we're dumping a boatload of fresh Kentucky manure on it. Hypothetically, you could declare under oath, heh-heh, oath – that tobacco doesn't cause cancer. Let's say in thirty years, hypothetically, they start saying there is no heating of the planet through man-made causes or that solar power and tires that last a lifetime are possible. You just put out a commercial with an American flag waving and "The Battle Hymn of the Republic" playing in the background as an American soldier salutes saying that it's all a hate-filled conspiracy against the troops and the American public will (hysterical laughter)… buy it. They'll buy anything.

Murdoch: What about setting up absurd certainties like say, I don't know… enrich the rich even more so that it will help the middle class and poor?

Nixon. Yes. And we can call it "fuck-the-poor-pricks" economics.

Erlichman: Too on the money.

Nixon: You're right. How about "Trick el clowns economics?"

Haldeman: Too Hispanic.

Murdoch: I got it. "Trickle-down economics."

Nixon: Nah. No one would buy it.

Murdoch: But if we could follow up with misnomers like "The Clean Air" act to fuck up the environment we might be able to get the public to believe anything.

Nixon: Rupe. You're always thinking like a fox. Do you think you can make the public believe there is no man-made destruction of the atmosphere even if, say, ninety-five percent of scientists say so.

Murdoch: I could try.

Nixon: How about cutting voting rights and saying that it's to protect voting rights?

Murdoch: That's a toughy. Ah, what the fuck, I'm not an American. Sure.

Yakov Smirnoff (albeit an extremely young one): I love this country. In Russia, country loves you. Not really, but it's all I got.

Donald Trump: I still don't get it.

Nixon: Rosemary. Turn off the tape.

Woods: I just did.

Nixon: Are you sure it's off?

Woods: Four minutes ago. I'd bet your presidency on it.

Nixon: Good. So, anyone hear any good kike jokes lately.

CLICK.

Holy shit. It was the additional four minutes Larry and Richard told me about. Even more astonishing, not only was there an audiotape, but Nixon must have installed a video camera in the Oval Office. Wow. Nixon was our first multi-media president.

I stood there, overwhelmed by what I had just heard. It was the Holy Grail. The no longer missing four minutes revealed something so onerous, so vicious, so unbelievable that you would only expect to find it in some fictional work. This was more than a cover-up of the Watergate break-in.

Along with his henchman and some of the most powerful people in the world, the former president had sold the country a bill of goods to keep us in Vietnam so that he could hold onto the presidency. That wouldn't have happened if the voters had their wits about them. Nixon was willing to sell his soul and the American people down the Mekong River to stay in office.

Moreover, the same scum, the ones who each had more money than 10,000 poor people put together (if you had sufficient adhesive), wanted so much more that they were determined to literally slash the intelligence of the American people to get it. Even the country's legislators were in cahoots with these wealthy bastards because they were more than willing to trade in their integrity and regard for the public to increase their riches, power and station in life.

More shocking is that even with most of these people now dead and gone, the conspiracy continues, but now with a new and even more malicious group of conspirators.*[68]

---

68 *Consortium made up with heads of large corporations, TV/Radio infotainers, Rupert Murdoch, Baseball commissioner Rush Limbaugh, Karl Rove, Steven Bannon, The Waltons (Christy, S. Robson, Jim, Alice and John-Boy), (Every) Trump, Don Thompson (President and CEO McDonalds), Robert Murcer, Cigarette Companies, Pharmaceuticals, Energy (Petroleum) Companies (Koch Bros, Mobil, Exxon, Shell), i.e. WEALTHIEST PEOPLE IN THE WORLD. Lest I forget, McDonald's fake founder, Ray Kroc, who I found out after watching "The Founder" (the story of how that prick ripped off the real founders of McDonalds), that Kroc was a royal prick.*

CHAPTER FORTY-SIX

It All Came Down to This

Vinci sputtered. No comprehensible words, He gathered himself.

"Very clever, Mr. Young. I guess you think yourself to be very smart. Sure, we made our money and wielded our power to lie, cheat and steal. But that was far too risky. So, instead we found it much easier to get rid of anyone who gave Americans any credit for intellect and replaced them with shallow beings who were willing to put on the most watered-down programming. In that way our words, products, pharmaceuticals, policies and marketing will seem to be in the best interest of… us. As a result, we have ultimate control over every American household."

"Not the entire world?" I sarcastically asked.

"We're trying," said Vinci. "And we'll stop at nothing to reach our objective. World domination."

It was time to go for the jugular.

"Then you were the one who ordered the killings of the writers?"

"I can't take all the credit," said a broadly smiling Vinci, as he waved his hand referring to the surrounding group. "How many of you were behind our… cleansing of the audiences' pallets?"

One by one they raised a hand.

"All of you?"

"Yes, all of us," they cheered as if they were a high school pep squad.

I pulled my spare cell phone out of my pocket.

"Thank you all," I said, glowing with a glorious sensation I had never felt before. I think they call it "success." I had 'em!

I pushed "play."

"Everything you just admitted was recorded with a copy sent directly to the Beverly Hill Celebrity Task Force. Your gig is up."

The room we were in was often used as a community meeting room. I ran to a podium at the front of the room where I found a microphone. I raised it high, then dropped it. It landed on my foot. Still, what a close.

Vinci grabbed my phone and pushed play. What played was muffled beyond any recognition. My pocket had muted the recording.

Vinci and his cohorts broke into uncontrollable laughter.

"Nice," said Vinci through his laughter.

Fuck.

Recommendation: If you're using a mic drop you better make sure your last joke actually worked.

"Steven, Steven, Steven," repeated Vinci, as he pulled out a pistol. "It seems like we have your answer."

He cocked his pistol. This was it. I wouldn't even have time for my life to flash before me. I hoped he would miss but I figured he had a couple more bullets just in case.

BAM!

A shot rang out. Didn't feel anything. Did he miss? I looked down at my body. No blood. No pain. He did miss... I thought. Better, when I looked up it was Vinci who had been hit, *bulleted* as it were. He was standing there holding his bleeding, formerly gun-holding hand. In the doorway stood the last people I expected to see. Well, there were probably a lot of people, many of them I didn't even know, who I didn't expect to see, but it was an expression that seemed apropos.

In the doorway, holding a smoking rifle, was Frank Rich alongside the extremely tall Bill O'Reilly.

"So," said O'Reilly through a wry smile. "We meet again."

"Asshole," declared Vinci wincing from the bullet to his hand. "We've never met."

"I was speaking to Mr. Young."

"Um… hi," I said, not sure whether O'Reilly saved my life or just prolonged my misery.

"I don't know if I've ever admitted to a mistake," conceded O'Reilly. "Mostly because I'm pretty sure I've never made one."

O'Reilly looked about the room as if he believed he had just made a hysterical comment, surely expecting laughter. Maybe a few smiles. None were forthcoming.

"Yes, but, um, it looks like I might have made my first one… about you, Mr. Young."

Nice save.

To say I was surprised would be an understatement.

"Thank you."

"I said 'might,'" corrected O'Reilly, sternly.

Alrighty. Thought it best that I stopped with my ongoing commentary.

"Mr. Vinci. I heard every word you and the rest of your *former* big shots had to say. I'd say your *controlling the world* days are over."

"I don't think so," came a weakened but serious voice.

Michael Ztivo, drenched in blood, his head slightly asunder, with one bleeding bullet hole perfectly situated between his eyes, held a pistol to the back of O'Reilly's head. He had neatly positioned another pistol to the back of Rich's head.

How Ztivo survived being shot continues to be a mystery to the medical world as well as to Disney World. Best anyone has been able to explain was that the complete absence of conscience or soul allowed space enough for the bullet to pass through his skull hitting nothing but the skull*[69].

"Good job, Michael," said a relieved Vinci as he took one of the pistols from Ztivo. "Looks like this isn't going to end well for any of you."

Vinci placed the pistol at my forehead. This was becoming a bit tedious. As they say in many a story, "it all came down to this." As I attempted to swallow a grapefruit-sized lump in my throat, I heard the trigger being pulled back.

BAM! BAM! BAM!

"Ah-h-h-h!" I screamed.

Volleys of gun fire filled the room. To my ever-lovin' disbelief, not one pierced moi.

But, one of them there shots, AGAIN, knocked the pistol out of Vinci's hand.

"GODDAMNIT!" screamed Vinci. "This is getting ridiculous."

Spotting a splattering of human remains that once was Michael Ztivo, I hypothesized there would not be one more word from the former, most powerful, Hollywood power broker. Felled by some dozen bullets (yes, I took the time to count), his enormous, fat head was completely blown off. I seriously doubted that he would be making another stunning comeback.

As the gun smoke cleared, a look around the room revealed what at first appeared to be the closing scene of a Tarantino film.

I would have been terrified if I just wasn't so ball-bustin' confused.

Standing around the room, smoking Ak-47s resting in their hands were (remember how I wrote that the last people I expected were Frank Rich and Bill O'Reilly. Well, this time, these people were the *lastest* I

---

69 *The skull, while an important factor in supporting the face and hair, is neither an organ nor a necessity for the body to survive. In fact, the skull-less natives of North Bangor, Maine are known to live into their nineties. Still, they are not easily approachable as they have a nasty reputation for being cruel dudes (but they are good in bed).*

expected to see) James Brooks, Charlie Kaufman, Chuck Lorre, Matt Groenig, David Kelley, Ricky Gervais and Richard Lewis. In front of them all – Larry David.

Freakin', F-in and most of all, Fucking, Larry David.

Wha-a-a-a-a?

"Pretty, pretty good job, Steve," said Larry.

I couldn't speak. My brain was straining to wrap its cerebral cortex around the 30 billion neurons and, to a lesser extent, axons swirling wildly about within my cranium. It was as if a quick look up on Wikipedia had more complicated my understanding of how simple signal impulses were triggered than I had first learned from my Operation game.

"I see you're confused," said Larry.

"Yuh think?"

Everyone in the room (who was still alive) roared with laughter.

"Hey, Lewis," Larry said. "You want to explain to our friend?"

"No," replied Richard.

"Have a seat, Steve." said Larry as he wiped blood off a nearby chair.

Blood doesn't wipe off easily. It tends to smear.

"That's okay," I said. "I'll stand."

"It's a long story."

CHAPTER FORTY-SEVEN

The Long Story

As Larry had warned, his explanation was long, complex, shocking, – and might I add for the sake of book sales – thee most entertaining story in the history of books.

Due to space limitations and a fast-declining lack of ink, I won't be able to go into the specifics.

But take my word, what was once bewildering, now all made sense.

CHAPTER FORTY-EIGHT

So That I Don't Get a Bad Yelp Rating

(The Specifics)

"One thing I'm not clear on. Could you explain up how you're now all, um, unmurdered? I mean, didn't Ztivo wipe you guys out?"

"Well, that's how it might have appeared."

"Please. Explain the dying – not dying – thing."

"Simple. CGI. Computer-Generated Imagery," Larry said matter-of-factly.

"Jesus Christ, Larry. Chuck Lorre was missing half his body."

"Steve, have you ever seen *2012*?"

"The film or the year?"

Larry seemed miffed. It was a legitimate question. At this point I couldn't be sure of anything. Still, Larry ignored my question.

"Do you think the world was actually being destroyed in the film?"

"Well, if it wasn't for Joan Cusack."

"It was John Cusack," interjected Larry.

I thought it was really a trivial mistake. The Cusack clan does have some quirky similarities. You'd think they were brother and sister.

"What about Michael Ztivo? He stalked and… *looked* like he murdered everyone."

"Oh, Steven, Steven. Steven. You are adorable. Despite how powerful Michael Ztivo once was, in the weakened state he had been reduced to, he would do anything, nay, everything he was asked to do with the promise of regaining his clout."

"So, he became willing to kill?"

"Willing to *attempt* to kill," Larry corrected me. "When you are so malleable, there is no right, no wrong. You become blind to everything but the goal you covet."

"So… all the more reason to believe he would be willing to kill."

Larry smiled broadly.

"Are you that dumb? When you are so myopically focused, with no consideration for anything or anyone else…"

"But wasn't that exactly the way he was when he had the power?"

"Ah. Difference is, when you have the power, everyone will do your bidding. Everyone will believe anything you say. But most of all… Fellas…."

Larry motioned to the *formerly dead* writers.

"If you're the one in charge, that power eliminates the need for reason," they chanted in unison.

A killer harmony resonated with Richard Lewis' rich vibrato nailing the refrain.

"But if that power – the only reason people do what you want – evaporates," said Larry, "you not only have nothing, but you, yourself, are as soft as your lowest paid lackey once was."

"But records show he murdered all of you."

"Steve. Every so-called murder was a set up. We're fucking writers. We wrote the script. Every weapon, every bullet was provided by our prop guys. Every move was choreographed by our production managers. Every seeming victim was selected by our casting directors. Make-up did Oscar-winning work and since this wasn't a movie, even more amazing. Hell, we brought in Rich "Fucking" Baker*[70] for special effects. You ever hear of Steven Spielberg?*[71]"

"Sure." I said. "Very cool."

"Yeah, well, we couldn't get him, but still, our team was pretty damn impressive."

"I'll say," I said. (Heh-heh. I said that I said "say.")

"PHLEM thought Ztivo was their pawn when all the time he was ours."

"Did Ztivo know?"

"Nope."

"So, the killing of Ztivo and all the others who seem to be lying dead all over the floor… fake?"

"Oh, no," said Larry. "Not fake. They're dead."

"Ay. But I still don't get why me."

"The world has been under siege for years. Humanity itself has been undermined. People have been kept from achieving their dreams. And we needed a…um… a…um…."

"A dupe. You needed a dupe. You set me up."

"Don't discount what part you played."

"So, it's my fault?"

"Do you remember a while back when you wanted to do an interview with me?"

"Hmm. Hazy."

---

70 *RICH BAKER won seven Academy Awards for special effects, including such films as "An American Werewolf in London," "Ed Wood" and "Men in Black."*

71 *STEVEN SPIELBERG Really?*

"And at that time, you told me you were thinking about writing a stupid book about me canceling the interview at the last minute?"

"I don't think I seriously thought about writing a book. I mean, it wasn't a big deal to me that you canceled the interview at the last minute. Or that you agreed to another interview and canceled that one at the last minute too. Really, I didn't think twice about that."

"Hey. Didn't I mention that I thought you had some good comedy chops and in the future I would use you?"

"Hey, that's Hollywood. People say they'll use you *sometime* but don't really mean it. You don't expect people to keep their word."

"Well, that's not me."

"So… you're going to hire me?"

"I already have."

I figured Larry was gaslighting*[72] me. Gaslighting is a method of screwing with someone's head. Sometimes it's the technique manipulated by a sociopath. I'm not saying that Larry is a sociopath. Really, being a sociopath is so subjective. I'll leave that up to Larry's therapist.

"I'm missing something here."

Could it be that I was gaslighting myself? I don't know if that's even possible. Maybe if I had some sort of multiple personality disorder. I have issues but I'm pretty sure I'm not a schizophrenic. And so am I.

"I have to say, I don't remember working for you."

"Well, Steve," Larry said with a wry smile as he pulled out a binder. "You might want to take a look at this."

72 *The most credible reference source in the world, Wikipedia, says, gaslighting is a form of manipulation that seeks to sow seeds of doubt in a targeted individual or members of a group, hoping to make targets question their own memory, perception, and sanity. In the book, "The Sociopath Next Door", author Mary Stout wrote, "Sociopaths and narcissists frequently use gaslighting tactics. Sociopaths consistently transgress social mores, break laws, and exploit others, but typically also are convincing liars, sometimes charming ones, who consistently deny wrongdoing. Thus, some who have been victimized by sociopaths may doubt their own perceptions."*

The binder held a couple of contracts. One I recognized as a Writers Guild contract. The other was from AFTRA, the television and radio actors' guild. Most surprising was that my name was on both.

"What is this?"

"It's what I promised you."

"I don't understand."

"You're hiring me?"

"I already have."

"I don't understand"

"Read them."

I'm not a lawyer, though that had more to do with the fact that I was unable to graduate from high school than not having the skillset to become an outstanding partner with a high-profile, Wall Street law practice. But it didn't take Clarence Darrow to see that this contract described an HBO film that I would co-write with Larry David. The AFTRA contract had me, as an actor, appearing in the film or television special. The name of the film: *The Larry David Code.*

As confused as I was over the past hours, it wasn't near how bewildered I was at this very moment. I could not wrap my brain around what Larry was trying to pull off. Besides not making any sense, I had no memory of signing either of these agreements. At best they had to be bogus signatures.

"I'm sorry, but I have no idea what these are. While it's pretty cool to have anything that says I wrote something with you, I certainly didn't sign these."

"Steve, are you saying that I forged your signatures?"

I wanted to say "yes," but having anything that said I worked with Larry was incredibly powerful.

"Are you saying that you didn't come to my house posing as a People Magazine reporter?"

I sucked in a long sigh.

"Guilty. But…"

"No *buts* needed," he interrupted. "You did what you felt you had to do."

"Okay, I admit it. But I'm being honest with you. I don't remember signing these."

"Again… you don't remember coming to my house as a People reporter?"

NOTE: So that you, the reader, don't have to turn back to the page this reveal took place, let me copy and paste that page here:

"Before we do this, I need you to sign these," said Larry.

Larry presented a couple of legal-looking documents with everything covered other than areas for me to sign.

"What are these," I asked.

"Standard interview agreements. You know, making sure that you only use what we speak about for your article. Someone in my position needs to protect himself from being exploited."

"I…I wouldn't ever do anything that would harm you or your reputation."

"Yeah. Sure. That's why you'll sign these. Of course, if you don't want the interview…"

"No, no, no. I'll sign them. Where do I sign?"

Larry pointed to the signature blocks.

"I can't see what I'm signing to."

"Look, Steve. If you don't want to do the interview…"

He started to get up.

"No! Let me have those."

He laid them on the coffee table and I signed. Makes sense. Really, he's Larry David.

Damnit. He is Larry David. He was on to me from the very start.

"Okay. You knew I wasn't with *People* but what were the contracts about?"

"I might be a comedy writer. Some might say an icon. Well, a lot of people do. But we were, and still are, dealing with an issue that is undermining society and taking away our very right to choose. And there's nothing funny about that."

"But an HBO movie?"

"Documentary," Larry corrected me. "We needed evidence."

"A documentary? Are you now going to shoot a film about all this?"

"Not *going to.* We already shot it."

With a wipe of his hand, Larry revealed a seeming hologram some seven feet in the air. A hologram of a complete film crew: cameramen, soundmen, director, script supervisors and a best boy, all in front of a well-stocked Craft Services table.

"Is that real?"

"Bobby..." Larry yelled to the team in the hologram.

The director, Bobby, waved.

"Howya doin', Steve," shouted Bobby.

I couldn't even fathom how all this worked.

"So those guys were following me though all of this? How did you shoot things where I wasn't?"

"Good question."

Larry waved his hand revealing five more film teams appearing in holograms set in the air.

"Wow," I exclaimed. "The budget alone."

"Have you ever taken a look at my *Seinfeld* syndication deals?"

"No."

"Well, trust me. Budget is no problem."

"Let me get this straight. You knew from the very beginning what was going to happen."

"Well, we were never 100% sure. Just like everything else I've done. I write a treatment, a story, and then I trust my players to speak through their characters."

"Okay, but don't you usually give the actors an idea of the story?"

"Usually. This time, some knew, some didn't. Very Woody Allen. Got to admit, this one was a first-time thing for me. And quite a challenge. Not being sure how it would end was pretty daunting."

"Are you saying you didn't know if I would live or die?"

"Well, I had my fingers crossed."

"Fingers crossed?!"

"Yeah. And I really don't believe in that stuff, but I have to admit, there were times during the past few days that I actually crossed my fingers."

"That's what stood between me and death? Your fingers?"

"Crossed."

"You set me up to go through all this crap, including plenty of killings around the world."

"Some of which were real."

"And you filmed all of this?"

"Exactly," Larry said, surprised. "Thought you said you were confused."

"I could have been killed, for real."

"It's a chance we had to take."

"We? How about me?"

"Precisely why I gave you a lead credit."

"Great. So why did you sign me on as a co-writer?"

"A lot of what happened was based on where you took the, um, story."

"So… I not only helped saved the world, but I also wrote…"

"Co-wrote," corrected Larry.

"Co-wrote," I agreed, sheepishly.

Surprising, as angry as I was, I had a boner. Not one of those soft, over fifty-year-old, barely capable of penetrating a rotting, skinned canta-loupe, boner. I'm talking a pulsing, fourteen-year-old's rock hard, ICBM missile capable of drilling through the most resistant raw piece of liver, boner. I was a co-writer along with Larry David. Being that I survived I was beginning to see the positive side.

"So, what happens now? I mean once the public sees all this evi-dence, they'll see PHLEM for what it is. Right?"

"Unfortunately, it's not that easy."

"Are you serious? After all this?"

"This is just the start. You'll present the evidence. Show them the hologram. We'll edit and schedule the film. Probably get a booking on Rachel Maddow and Jon Stewart. Some will hear it. Less will believe it. But once we get this started the public will slowly begin to demand better programming, accept fewer shit products and political deception. They'll gradually get accustomed to quality programming. The most difficult chal-lenge will be that while we have eliminated many of the leaders of PHLEM, there are plenty more from the corporate and political worlds willing to step in and continue profiting from distortions and outright poisoning of society."

"So, I guess there's a lot more to do."

"A lot," Larry insisted.

I waited for more, but none was forthcoming. Larry and the others stood around, kibitzing with each other. Larry let out a long breath, shrugged his shoulders and began to walk away.

"Wait a minute," I said.

Larry stopped and turned towards me.

"That's it?" I asked

"That's it," Larry answered.

"After all this, the story ends here?"

"Oh, I don't know," said Larry. "There's always the possibility of a sequel."

"All right, folks." shouted Bobby, the cameraman. "That's a wrap. Nice job, everyone."

I was finished.

"But..."

Fade Out.

End

Oh, And…

History is always written by the winners. When two cultures clash, the loser is obliterated, and the winner writes the history books—books which glorify their own cause and disparage the conquered foe. As Napoleon once said, 'What is history, but a fable agreed upon?'" Dan Brown, *The Da Vinci Code*

EPILOGUE

With hope and the ability to innovate restored, Larry and I sat in a Studio City McDonald's Playplace sipping a cup of java. Unfortunately, not from the same cup.

This was the opportunity where I could ask a question I had wanted to ask Larry for years, a question that had originally instigated me wanting to write the story he had twice turned down and precipitated our remarkable odyssey.

"Look at those precious children," said the misty-eyed Larry. "Climbing the steps, crawling through the tubes and giggling down the slides. It warms my heart. No, wait a minute. That's the coffee. I've got to remember to let it sit."

"Larry, would you mind if I ask you a question?"

"Not at all. Whether I answer it is up in the air."

"Fair enough. What is your creative process like?"

Larry took a long breath. Longer than I believed was humanly possible. A lot longer. So long he began to turn blue. A beautiful shade. Not Smurf. More of a clear sky blue. Wait a minute. Now it's Smurf. Oh my God. He's choking. I jumped up, lifted him from his seat and wrapped my arms around him just under his chest. I pulled tight and Larry projectile-vomited out a half-chewed McNugget.

"'Thanks," said Larry, never letting credit where credit was due go unacknowledged.

"The creative process is like the peeling of an onion."

"Are we talking about pulling away the bullshit until deep within you discover absolute center, where the theme, the unambiguous reason the story must be written, sits?"

"What? No. I'm talking about the need to wear protective goggles so that you aren't brought to tears. Writing is where the emotion meets the mental, struggling to generate something new, unique and hopefully entertaining to someone other than your mother. That struggle can and most often causes the writer to sob uncontrollably. It's fundamentally impossible to write with tears in your eyes. You can't see the page. If an exceptionally potent onion, you could end up soaking the keyboard causing a malfunction that will distract even the most focused writer from creating an original piece of work. Without goggles, it's far more stressful to focus on your project. So, you place the goggles on and voila… success."

And with that, he took a sip of coffee, placed it on the table and stood up. He gave me one of those Larry smiles that just melts your heart. I figured, if I don't ask now, I'll never get a better opportunity.

"Larry, can I… can I write on your next show?"

His smile grew from a smirk into an open-mouthed howl of laughter, evolving into cackling that I first thought he might be choking on another McNugget. I jumped up and tried to wrap my arms just below his chest. He pushed me away, still laughing.

"No. No. I'm alright," he said still grasping for breath. "You are so funny."

And off he walked, shaking his head. The spotlight that followed him shrunk ever smaller as he finally disappeared into the Abyss… or maybe a Prius. I never get those car models right.

A content smile crossed my face.

He didn't say "no."

And… scene.